Public Private Partnerships in Middle East Development:
The Challenge of Civil Society Engagement

Alexandra De Vito, M.C.R.P.
John M. B. Balouziyeh, J.D.

Public Private Partnerships in Middle East Development:
The Challenge of Civil Society Engagement

ISBN (13) (paperback): 978-1-68109-002-3
ISBN (10) (paperback): 1-68109-002-3
ISBN (13) (Kindle): 978-1-68109-003-0
ISBN (10) (Kindle): 1-68109-003-1
ISBN (13) (ePub): 978-1-68109-004-7
ISBN (10) (ePub): 1-68109-004-X

Time Books™
an imprint of TellerBooks™
TellerBooks.com/Time_Books

t TellerBooks

www.TellerBooks.com

Manufactured in the U.S.A.

TABLE OF CONTENTS

ACKNOWLEDGEMENTS

We wish to thank our parents and families for their unfailing support and our professors at the University of Texas, Regent University, and the Institute of Political Studies of Paris, who have broadened our understanding. We are grateful for their contribution to our education. We wish to thank friends and colleagues at Corgan Associates, Inc. for their patience and encouragement, and at the US Department of State, for their support throughout our research, as well as the American Institute for Yemeni Studies, for supporting this research.

ABBREVIATIONS

CLT	Community Land Trust
CWRAS	Country Water Resource Assistance Strategy
DS	Dudley Street
DSNI	Dudley Street Neighborhood
GDP	Gross Domestic Product
GTZ	*Deutsche Gesellschaft für Technische Zusammenarbeit* (German Development Corporation)
HDI	Human Development Index
IBRD	International Bank for Reconstruction and Development
IHC	International Humanitarian City
IMF	International Monetary Fund
MEPI	U.S.-Middle East Partnership Initiative
NGO	Non-governmental organization
NWSA	National Water and Sanitation Authority (of Yemen)
NWSSIP	National Water Sector Strategy and Investment Program
PPP	Public Private Partnership
Riley Foundation	Mabel Louise Riley Foundation
Sana'a Local Corporation	Sana'a Water Supply and Sanitation Local Corporation
UAE	United Arab Emirates
UN	United Nations

ABSTRACT

Public Private Partnerships in Middle East Development:
The Challenge of Civil Society Engagement

Alexandra De Vito, M.C.R.P.
John M. B. Balouziyeh, J.D.

Over the past sixty years, the field of international development has come full circle, returning to priorities that value people over gross domestic product. Principles for successful development, such as institution building, managed competition to reduce corruption, human organization, the design of solutions to fit problems and social, political and economic stability, have also emerged throughout the international development literature. Building on this foundation, this book proposes the use of public-private partnerships as a tool for implementing development practice in the Middle East and analyzes the challenges that stand in the way of effective partnerships between governments and civil society.

PART 1.
GENERAL OVERVIEW

Chapter 1.

INTRODUCTION TO THE PROBLEM

International development is field that has been plagued by a mix of mostly unpredicted successes and failures. The field has progressed more by trial and error than by any sophisticated engineering. Emerging out of World War II's aftermath, the young international development institutions of the capitalist world, battling against communist aggression in poor defenseless countries, began eagerly supporting former colonies that had gained independence. Armed with economic models that were sure to work, these institutions fully expected to eradicate poverty, to establish global stability, and thereby make the world a better place.

Sixty years later, the international development community, after experiencing multiple failures of theory in practical application, has significantly evolved, having learned lessons and developed best practices. Its earlier self-assurance has been replaced by circumspection. Although the international development literature has come to advocate a more sensitive approach to development, focusing on people as the most important element of any development strategy, international development practice is still learning to implement development planning procedures that conform to this doctrine.

A series of recommendations for focusing on people as the center of development initiatives has emerged in the international development literature. These recommendations are widely agreed upon by practitioners, yet the international development apparatus has nonetheless been stuck halfway between entrenched procedures that reinforce statism and newer methods that focus on empowering people. The standard procedures used in international development practice are slow to change from a top-down approach that reinforces statism to a bottom-up approach that empowers people.

Public private partnerships (hereinafter, "PPPs") are a flexible means of creating contractual agreements between public and private organizations. Although they are being widely used in international development practices, PPPs are more often oriented towards privatization within the international development context than towards empowering citizens.

This thesis proposes the use of PPPs in international development as a means of implementing the recommendations of international development literature, thereby advancing international development practice toward successful and responsible actions. After reviewing the literature supporting recommended principles for successful development in Chapter 2 and studying freedom as it relates to development in Chapter 3, the assumption that PPPs could be used in international development practice to implement literature recommendations will be tested by studying three public private partnership cases in Chapter 4. These cases will be studied for how the partnerships implemented or did not implement recommended principles for successful development. Finally, in Chapter 5, the potential for PPPs as an effective tool in international development practice to implement successful development principles will be asserted, with a series of recommendations for their application.

Chapter 2.

DEVELOPMENT THEORY AND LITERATURE
REVIEW

"The growth and development of people is the highest calling of leadership."
Harvey S. Firestone[1]

International development theory has moved full circle from the end of World War II to the late 1990s. In the early days after the War, development was directed in the Marshall Plan by business, academic, agricultural and private finance leaders. Yet what began as a process guided by a real understanding of problems and people eventually transformed into a mathematical formula for foreign aid input to economic growth output. By the 1950s, a new group of technocrats and economists in the Bretton Woods Institutions emerged as the leaders in development. The 1950s through the 1990s gave rise to a rapidly shifting and ever changing theories and development models, continually evolving to explain persistent poverty in light of numerous economic failures. These failures eventually gave way to the return of process-oriented development, where the concept of GDP has been replaced by the concept of people, a change that represents a significant advance for humanity.

---

[1] American industrialist founder of the Firestone Tire & Rubber Co., 1868-1938.

General Overview

2.1   The Marshall Plan

At the conclusion of the Second World War, in 1945, Europe was in physical and economic ruin. Whatever industrial equipment had survived the destruction of the war was antiquated. Industrial manufacturing had come to a complete halt. While there was an abundance of overvalued European currency, there was little to buy. This led to extreme inflation and, subsequently, to the hoarding of gold and dollars. Farmers in Italy and France were growing less than fifty percent of their normal crop because there was no incentive to sell crops for money when there was no farming equipment available for purchase.[2] By 1947, Europe was on the brink of starvation.

Although the United States had already spent an estimated $9 billion between 1945 and 1947 in food through the United Nations, the situation in Europe was not improving.[3] It became apparent to some in Washington, as expressed by Secretary of State George Marshall in his Harvard University commencement address on June 5, 1947, that the United States should take an active role in restoring political stability to Europe by pursuing comprehensive economic reconstruction.[4] Following a great

---

[2] Dulles, Allen (1994) *The Marshall Plan.* Berg Publishers.

[3] *Ibid.*

[4] "It is logical that the United States should do whatever it is able to do to assist in the return of normal economic health in the world, without which there can be no political stability and no assured peace. Our policy is directed not against any country or doctrine but against hunger, poverty, desperation, and chaos. Its purpose should be the revival of a working economy in the world so as to permit the emergence of political and social conditions in which free institutions can exist. Such assistance, I am convinced, must not be on a piecemeal basis as various crises develop. Any assistance that this Government may render in the future should provide a cure rather than a mere palliative. Any government that is willing to assist in the task of recovery will find full cooperation, I am sure, on the part of the United States Government."

Taken from Speech Delivered by General George Marshall at Harvard University on June 5, 1947. Modern History Sourcebook, Nov. 09, 2008, available at http://www.fordham.edu/halsall/mod/1947marshallplan1.html.

campaign aimed at converting Congress and ensuing visits to Europe by over two hundred members of the Senate and the House, legislation approving the first year of the European Recovery Program was passed into law by December of 1947.

The European Recovery Program, which would later come to be known as the "Marshall Plan," focused on the people of Europe as the source of their own hope. If the threat of famine could be eliminated, then European society could convert itself into a system of production, positioning itself to return as an active member in the global economy. Within the context of this focus, or "theme," the Marshall Plan had four main goals: (1) to bring humanitarian aid to Europe and to halt starvation; (2) to help Europe recover so that it could purchase American goods; (3) to contain communism; and (4) to demonstrate that free, open economies work. Before reviewing the details of how these goals were met, it is important to understand what was perceived as the problem behind Europe's troubles.

It was no secret that President Truman held opposed colonialism.[5] He actively promoted a policy of encouraging Europe to free all of its colonies, which were considered to be the source of inter-European wars. Europe had long been dominated by nationalism and had overemphasized sovereignty relative to economic efficiency. For example, European nations, rather than trade with one another, frequently traded with only their respective colonies. Resulting from American fatigue of European wars that stemmed from an overemphasis on sovereignty, the Marshall Plan sought to create economic interdependence by promoting intra-European trade, such that future wars in Europe would be rendered impossible.

The Marshall Plan thus made European nations less dependent on their colonies and more dependent on one another

---

[5] McKinzie, Richard D. 1974. "Oral History Interview with John Wesley Jones." Harry S. Truman Library & Museum, Nov. 9, 2008, available at http://www.trumanlibrary.org/oralhist/jonesjw.htm.

through trade. Changes in trade patterns and tariffs were central to the requirements of the Plan, which responded directly to the perceived root cause of wars in Europe by redesigning the economic system by which intergovernmental relationships were forged. Although the Plan had many goals, this systemic change built from Europe's existing capacity for economic production persisted as a thread throughout the implementation of the Plan and the realization of its goals.

As the United States began considering the challenges of reconstruction, three criteria emerged for evaluating potential strategies: (1) the capability of the United States to contribute resources without stunting its own capacity for economic growth;[6] (ii) the European situation as assessed by independent American sources; and (iii) how the United States could most effectively administer aid to maximize assistance in Europe while protecting the American economy.[7]

It was decided that first, the most urgent and basic need in Europe, food, would be exported to avert the starvation crisis. Second, incentives were created for European farmers to boost food production, which presented a more sustainable solution to the food shortage. Once the foot shortage was curbed, urban Europeans could move into industry, producing their own goods and services and rebuilding their own economies. It was also important that the currency be stabilized to stop inflation, which was imperative in creating a climate for investment and growth.

The Plan eventually evolved into two programs: (1) the emergency aid program; and (ii) the reconstruction and capital goods program. The former provided grants, while the latter provided capital goods via loans. The items slated for grant status were goods that are rapidly consumed. Additionally, the

---

[6] It should be noted that the total United States contribution equaled $22 billion over a four year period, which was less than three percent of the United States national income during the lifespan of the program.

[7] Dulles, Allen (1994) *The Marshall Plan.* Berg Publishers.

determination of what would be supplied through a grant versus a loan depended upon each individual country's ability to repay and the effect of dept accumulation on its recovery.

In the emergency aid program, primary United States assistance was given to the agricultural sector in food to feed the farmers and stabilize the currency, encouraging the farmers to sow their seed and not to eat it. Food, fuel, and fertilizer, which made up seventy percent of the total aid provided, were provided in the form of grants. The provision of tools to help Europeans to increase their own production of food, fuel and fertilizer was also in the form of grants. All aid was provided in-kind rather than in cash, since: (1) dollars were useless for food; and (2) the United States, by purchasing American goods for export to Europe, benefited its own economy while avoiding competition from foreign countries.

The reconstruction and capital goods program (the second program of the Marshall Plan), provided loans only for capital and commodities that would directly increase productivity and create the means by which the loans would be repaid. Consequently, the industrial sector was mostly rebuilt through loans. In rebuilding the European industrial sector, private American business played a substantial role relative to that of the American government, whose intervention was limited. Many American businesses gave machinery and needed capital to rebuild European factories through partnerships, whereby American businesses would then own part of the European counterpart. Most of the capital was provided through loans that were managed by either the World Bank, the Export-Import Bank, or by private institutions. Intergovernmental loans were avoided under the reasoning that the loan should be handled by one of the above-mentioned institutions, "if the credit of the borrower [was] good enough to justify calling for repayment in dollars."[8] In order to encourage private capital, the federal government set aside dollars to cover any costs incurred

---

[8] Dulles, Allen (1994) *The Marshall Plan*. Berg Publishers.

in transferring a debtor's assets into dollars; however, the government was not to underwrite the ordinary risks of business.

The implementation of the Plan was perhaps the strongest means of restructuring the economic system of Europe from colonialism to regional interdependence. The sixteen nations that participated in the program agreed to commit themselves to: "(1) the creation and maintenance of internal financial stability; (2) the development of economic cooperation to bring production to the specific targets, especially in the cases of food and coal; (3) cooperation in the reduction of tariffs and trade barriers; and (4) organization of the means by which common resources can be developed in partnership."[9] The participating nations were required to submit their deficits and then to coordinate amongst one another as to how they would help each other before the United States would provide assistance. For example, Italy, which might have had an excess of vegetables, but a shortage of coal, could trade with Germany, which might have an excess of coal, but no food. From this emerged the Organization for European Economic Co-operation, which provided the organizational vehicle for all sixteen participating nations to negotiate and prepare a plan for their own recovery. American aid would only be provided once this plan had been coordinated. This created the institutional framework for managed competition.

Additionally, participating nations were required to "deposit in a special account the amount of local currency equivalent to the aid furnished in the form of grants."[10] These deposits would be used in a manner mutually agreed upon by the United States and the country concerned. These countries were also to provide full information regarding how the aid was put to use, establishing the pattern for public open transparent regulation. Even with all of these conditions, the United States retained the right to discontinue assistance at its sole discretion.

[9] *Ibid.*
[10] Dulles, Allen (1994) *The Marshall Plan.* Berg Publishers.

Development Theory and Literature Review

In considering the unique aspects of the Marshall Plan, it might be worth mentioning that George Marshall never planned the reconstruction of Europe. Rather, he proposed a process by which the participating European nations planned their own economic recovery. What is also unique about the Plan is that it responded directly to real problems with the comprehensive approach of a designer rather than with a model copied from an abstract theory. The problem of eliminating future European wars was addressed by altering the system by which the relationships among the European nations were created. The problem of starvation, inflation, and economic recovery were addressed by a multi-phased process of first providing food for people in the form of grants, then providing grants for agricultural production equipment, and third, providing industrial capital goods in the form of loans after currency stabilization took place.

Another unique aspect of the Plan is that it created an economic incentive for people to organize themselves and to coordinate their respective activities. The United States did not coordinate this organizing; it merely provided the carrot by promising aid once all parties had negotiated an agreement. The coordination and competition created among the donees necessarily created a system of checks and balances in authenticating each nation's statement of need and their proposed allocation of United States aid. The possibility of corruption was further repelled by requiring public open transparent disclosure in how the aid was used. At the time of the Marshall Plan, Europe had a significant level of human capital. The Plan relied completely on the people of Europe to make reconstruction a success, and there are few who would say it did not meet its goals.

2.2   Establishment of the Bretton Woods Institutions

At the same time that Europe was entering the last nine months of World War II, a new global system of monetary management was being established in Bretton Woods, New

Hampshire. While the express purpose of the Bretton Woods Agreement was to require signing nations to regulate the exchange rate of their currency to facilitate the stability required for free trade, it also gave birth to two institutions that have become the hope and disappointment of international development: the World Bank and the International Monetary Fund (hereinafter, "IMF"). The IMF's original mission was to ensure global economic stability by pressuring countries that were not "doing their fair share to maintain global aggregate demand, by allowing their own economies to go into a slump."[11] The IMF, when necessary, would also provide liquidity in the form of loans to those countries that, due to economic downturns or crises, were unable to stimulate aggregate demand with their own resources.

The World Bank Group was originally one bank known as the "International Bank for Reconstruction and Development" (hereinafter, "IBRD"). It has since grown to a group of five institutions, of which IBRD is a member. The purpose in creating the bank was to finance the reconstruction of Europe. However, the young institution did not have the credit resources to deal with the magnitude of Europe's reconstruction. Additionally, the IBRD bonds could only be sold on Wall Street, as it was the only market available for such bonds. At the time, conservative Wall Street banking forced the IBRD to behave likewise and only grant loans when repayment was guaranteed. The Marshall Plan eventually addressed the issue of Europe's reconstruction, mostly through grants. Since the original mission of the IBRD was never realized, it has since shifted its mission to fight poverty by financing governments.

---

[11] Stiglitz, Joseph E. 2003. *Globalization and Its Discontents.* W. W. Norton & Company.

Development Theory and Literature Review

2.3 Survey of Development Theory and Strategies Since the Marshall Plan

After the establishment of the Bretton Woods Institutions, the face of international development changed. The institutions that came to take a central role in development — the IMF and the World Bank — were dominated by economists, whereas the earlier Marshall Plan was spearheaded by a diverse committee that included representatives from steel and agriculture organizations; synthetic rubber, shipping, and coal interests; private foreign exchange and international investment banks; skilled labor; the Federal Reserve Bank; policy experts; and electric, chemical, automotive, and academic organizations.[12] It is no wonder that for forty years, between the end of the Marshall Plan and the early 1990s, international development has been conducted by technocrats armed with theories that are yet to produce a case as intensely successful as the Marshall Plan.

In this section, a survey of the development theories that have characterized the international development field from the 1950s to 1990s will be presented.

2.3.1 Forced Savings

Forced savings was first articulated by Henry Thornton in 1804. At around the time of the Second World War, it reentered modern discussion of economic theory among economists such as John Maynard Keynes[13] and Ludwig von Mises.[14] The theory held that people are more likely to consume their income and cannot be trusted to invest. Therefore, forced suppression of consumption produces forced savings that ultimately can then be invested.

Government may suppress consumption by increasing inflation by means of printing more money and shifting resources

---

[12] Dulles, Allen (1994) *The Marshall Plan*. Berg Publishers.

[13] Keynes, John Maynard. 1940. *How to Pay for the War*. London

[14] Mises, Ludwig von. 1934. *Theory of Money and Credit*. London.

away from consumer goods production (thus lowering quantities), which increase the prices of consumer goods. With newly printed money, the government may invest in capital goods. The new money causes higher prices and consequently, households can no longer consume the same amount of goods. The result is suppressed consumption, forced savings and investment in the form of capital goods.

Governments might also pursue a tax policy that reflects the assumption of forced savings economic theory that people cannot be trusted to invest. Thus, the government suppresses consumption through high taxes, which restrict income in order to force the transfer of savings into the government's control. Government then takes upon itself the burden of investing on behalf of society.

One criticism of forced savings is that inflation disrupts society and the burden of inflation is not evenly shared. After World War II, many less developed countries in Latin American applied forced saving policies in order to finance economic development.[15] Unfortunately, the policies were not successful in creating economic development, as the savings were often invested in speculative real estate or some other type of investment with no real value to society. A second criticism is that if the private sector cannot produce the entrepreneurship to invest, there is very little reason to believe the public sector will. A third criticism is of the basic assumption that in order to stimulate investment, consumption must be suppressed. This third criticism suggests that consumption is actually a form of investment in production. The most simplistic example is that the consumption of food is an investment in the productivity of the physical body.

2.3.2 Take-Off Theory

Walt Whitman Rostow, an American economist, first published his take-off theory for economic development in 1956.

---

[15] Harris, Seymour Edwin. 1972. *Economic Problems of Latin America.*

Development Theory and Literature Review

He proposed that nations develop in a predictable pattern. First, certain preconditions exist where physical and institutional infrastructure is built up to support investment and growth. Second, the economy is suddenly stimulated into a take-off period by some intervening factor, such as a political revolution or a change or improvement in technology or production processes. Third, the economy endures a take-off period, whereby: (a) the rate of savings increases from five to ten percent; (b) one or more substantial manufacturing sectors develop with high growth due to domestic demand; and (c) there is a rapid expansion of political, social and institutional frameworks to take advantage of the stimulus and to mobilize capital. Finally, the national savings rate increases to more than ten percent and the economic growth and development is self-sustained.

Some of Rostow's assumptions regarding savings, investment and capital follow narrow definitions. According to Rostow, capital includes only three types of assets: (1) housing; (2) manufacturing plants and office buildings; and (3) major machinery or equipment. Investment is capital formation, which is the production of the above-listed forms of capital. Rostow did not view land as an investment. He assumed, rather, that investment occurred through such institutions as banks and stocks.

In analyzing the stages of economic development presented in his take-off theory, Rostow proposed that the vanguard, professional elites, not traditional elites concerned with preserving the status quo, cause the take-off, since they are more likely to be productive with capital. Consequently, he argues that the government should invest in the creation of a vanguard elite that can transform economies.

The primary critiques of Rostow's theory come from economic historians who argue that societies have always been characterized by both traditional and vanguard elites, which suggests that the existence of a entrepreneurial (vanguard) elite is not the magic key to economic transformation. Rather, proper infrastructure is more crucial to economic growth because without it, economic growth is unsustainable. They also argue that growth has been happening long before the industrial revolution. They question Rostow's urban bias by excluding land in his definition of capital and his assumption that development is always marked by industrialization and manufacturing. They also criticize his theory for promoting international development policies that were insensitive to cultural differences in assuming both a western industrial model of development and a vanguard elite with western ideals as universal.

2.3.3   Comparative Advantage

Comparative advantage theory grew as a major economic policy for development in less developed countries after World War II. The classical comparative advantage and trade theory of Adam Smith and David Ricardo holds that the growth of a national economy will accelerate on the specialization of productions and trade on which the nation has a comparative advantage. The classical comparative advantage theory assumes that only labor creates value and that all factors of production in the domestic economy are perfectly mobile and in perfect competition. The modern version of the comparative advantage theory, as it was conceived by Eli Heckscher and Bertil Ohlin in 1933, converted all aspects of the classical growth theory to cost.[16] The new theory revised the assumptions to include both labor *and* capital as factors that create value, and assumed that the basis of production, specialization and trade were production cost and opportunity cost.

Although the Smith-Ricardo classical growth theory of comparative advantage remains applicable to development strategies, the Heckscher-Ohlin model does it. It is merely a mathematical formula that nonetheless was applied in economic policy in the 1960s in less developed countries. This latter model of

---

[16] Chenery, H. B. 1961. Comparative Advantage and Economic Policy.

comparative advantage suggested that the advantage in trade lies in the cost of labor: if a nation had low cost labor in one sector, it should export goods produced by that sector; but if it had a high labor cost in a sector, it should import products of that sector. Once it could be determined from past production costs which country could produce certain items at a lower cost than others, relative ratios of productivity could be compared to determine how to reach maximum global productivity for the same cost. This information could then be used to inform resource allocation decisions to build up certain sectors in specific nations.

The main critique of applying the Heckscher-Ohlin model to economic development policy is that it suggests developing a central planning agency to run the global economy using its maximum productivity charts as the basis for who receives investment. This would disrupt the existing social, economic and political order. Another critique is that by basing the cost comparison ratios on past production costs, it does not reflect real life future risks, which should temper resource allocation decisions. Another critique is that the conversion of the classical comparative advantage theory into a model of costs, where labor is a measure of cost, reflects an industrial urban bias. A farmer's labor is not counted in the Heckscher-Ohlin model. This new model of comparative advantage, particularly when applied to economic development policy, has notably departed from the classical Smith-Ricardo growth theory.

2.3.4 Gap Financing: Harrod Domar Growth Model

The Harrod Domar growth model was developed independently by Sir Roy F. Harrod in 1939 and Evsey Domar in 1946. Without getting into the details of the calculations, the model suggests that output (or income) is a function of capital. It predicts that the output over a period of time will be the previous year's net investment in GDP, or that GDP growth will be proportional to the share of investment spending in GDP.

General Overview

This model was applied to development policy as a means of justifying foreign aid investment. The model suggests that growth is a factor of investment, but development experts usually discussed it in terms of how much investment is required to meet a *desired* level of growth. The Incremental Capital Output Ratio (ICOR) represents the ratio of required investment to desired growth for a particular country. For example, if a country has an investment rate of four percent, and an ICOR of four, then its investment rate of four dividing by the ICOR ratio of four predicts that growth will be one percent, which would not keep up with a population growth rate of two percent. If the target economic growth rate is three percent, then the gap in investment is equal to eight percent.[17] In an environment of heightened Cold War fears, wealthy capitalist nations were persuaded to finance the investment gap in poor nations. This gap financing model was in competition with Soviet foreign investment raised through forced savings.

The Harrod Domar model fell out of fashion to the Solow growth model in the 1970s and 1980s because it had not produced the economic growth that it predicted. Critics argued that resource *allocation* was more important than resource quantity. However, counterarguments supporting the use of the model continued through the 1990s, suggesting that gap financing was *necessary* though not *sufficient* for economic growth.[18]

Those who oppose any use of the model argue that the idea that there is a ratio of input to output is not based on reality. It is inconceivable that an entrepreneur could run a business using a model of input-output ratios, considering there are multiple factors significant to growth which are not included in the model, such as human capital. Other critics have pointed out that gap financing puts money into the problem without really understanding the

---

[17] Easterly, W. 1997. The Ghost of Financing Gap: How the Harrod Domar Growth Model Still Haunts Development Economic.

[18] *Ibid.*

16

problems in a country. Perhaps one country requires machines and another requires cell phone technology. This approach to development provides money to governments, suggesting that private sectors lack the skills to invest resources successfully. As a final criticism, the model does not recognize the importance of institutions to sustainable growth.

2.3.5   Surplus Labor

In the 1950s, Sir William Arthur Lewis proposed a return to the classical labor surplus model in pursuing development strategies in less developed countries. Marxist economics define surplus labor as labor that is unpaid or uncompensated by a wage. This is the source of the capitalist's profit. The classical labor surplus model developed during the first industrial revolution in the eighteenth century, as the migration of labor from the rural agricultural sector to the urban industrial sector resulted in economic growth.

Since agriculture is seasonal, surplus labor theorists assumed that people in the agricultural sector only work seasonally and remain unemployed for over fifty percent of the year. The wages of a farm hand were considered greater than the marginal return for his labor because he was doing nothing productive during most of the year (this is termed, "disguised unemployment"). The classical labor surplus model assumed that the elastic flow of unemployed labor from the countryside to the cities maintained stable low wages for factory workers. Stable low wages, a result of elastic labor, produced a labor surplus, resulting in higher profits for capitalists.[19]

Lewis' return to the classical surplus labor model was propelled by development economists in the 1950s and 1960s. If the disguised unemployment in the agricultural sector could be

---

[19] Williamson, Jeffrey G. 1985. The Historical Content of the Classical Labor Surplus Model.

transferred to year-round full-time employment in industrial factories, it would propel the economy into accelerated growth. It would also induce greater efficiency into the agricultural sector while maintaining low wages in the industrial sector, increasing capital and overall economic growth. This encouraged disinvestment in agriculture, which was perceived as inefficient, and encouraged new investment in industry.

Governments applied this theory to policy through price controls. They would control the market by purchasing food from farmers at low prices and selling the food to the urban population at market price. The profit often amounted to a tax of nearly fifty one percent on the production of farmers. This profit was in turn used to fund the expansion of the industrial sector. The government would squeeze the farmers and push migration from rural areas to urban centers.

The critique of the application of the surplus labor model to development policy is that it failed to understand agrarian economics. Farmers do not always concern themselves with increasing profits; rather, they focus on reducing costs. If they can produce something themselves for less than they can purchase it, they will. Furthermore, what has been perceived as seasonal unemployment in the agricultural sector by economists with an urban bias is often a time of investment in the farm. During off-seasons, machinery is mended, irrigation systems are repaired, and other forms of preparation for more active seasons in farming are conducted. Additionally, it has been proven that more labor in the agriculture sector results in higher productivity.[20] Labor is critical to the harvest and planting seasons. If labor is encouraged to migrate to the industrial urban centers, it may result in lowering agricultural productivity and may force the government to import food that was once domestically produced. The increase in

---

[20] Ranis, Gustav. 2004. Arthur Lewis' Contribution to Development Thinking and Policy. Yale University, available at http://www.rh.edu/~stodder/BE/Lewis_byRanis.htm.

industrial production is countered by a decrease in agricultural production and does not produce overall economic growth, as the theory suggests.

Critics of the surplus labor model also contend that real development involves a division of labor, where urban labor is interdependent with farmers and other rural labor. Agriculture is freed by technology, allowing those who would have worked on the farm to be free to work in industry, manufacturing the technology that farmers are using to replace labor. While it is a concern that work once realized by people is now realized by machines running on petroleum and other non-renewable resources that will become depleted, the division of labor is a mark of real development, and is contrary to the surplus labor model, which suggests that agriculture has embedded within it hidden unemployment.

2.3.6 *Washington Consensus*

More commonly know as "Reaganomics," the Washington Consensus represented a major shift in policy for both domestic and international development in the 1980s. By this point in history, many central planning strategies had failed to reduce global poverty. With the evidence that China provides, we now know that central planning in itself is not the source of these failures. The recent credit crisis of 2008 in the United States similarly shows a market failure where government intervention cannot be blamed, since the government only intervened after the crisis in mortgage-backed securities arose. However, it was the economic development strategies prior to 1980 that promoted government intervention in markets *through price controls* and suppression of market demand (such as in the extreme case of the Soviet Union, though many capitalist nations also followed these growth strategies) that had destroyed competition and efficiency, and had failed to produced economic growth.

General Overview

This set the stage for the three pillars of the Reagan-Thatcher Washington Consensus: privatization, liberalization, and macrostability. Privatization is based on the principle that market forces are better at providing certain goods and services than can the government, which should instead focus its attention on its essential functions without being sidetracked with tasks that are more efficiently executed by the private sector. Liberalization, a direct reaction against central planning and government interventionist policies, discourages any government intervention in financial and capital markets through trade barriers and other regulations. It is based on the idea that capital should flow freely within and between countries and governments should allow market forces to regulate themselves. Macrostability seeks to create the right environment for foreign investment through currency exchange and controlling for inflation.

These policies brought a mixture of success and failure to economies around the globe. The central critique of the Washington Consensus aims at its poor implementation record. The Structural Adjustment Programs of the IMF, which were meant to establish the climate for growth for nations in economic crises, painted a picture of how things *ought* to be without planning for how a country would transition smoothly to that end. For example, if a government was subsidizing an inefficient nationalized industry, it was told to sell it off to the private sector. There was no thought given as to whether sufficient regulatory institutions and laws, such as anti-trust laws or environmental protections, were in place to protect the public. There was furthermore no transparency or oversight for assuring the national industries were not sold below cost to friends and supporters of those who held political power.

In the Washington Consensus model, nations were ordered to open up their financial markets so that foreign capital could be freely invested therein. The principle of open financial markets might seem like a means of encouraging investment and economic growth, but the details of how a nation with closed financial markets transitioned to open markets made the difference as to whether the principle actually worked. In many instances, when a nation's financial markets were suddenly opened, they attracted a great deal of short-term capital investments that were speculating on changes in currency values. The net effect of these short-term capital investments, which were quickly withdrawn from local economies, was to destabilize financial market and to thus discourage the long-term capital needed for development strategies with long gestation periods.

Countries were also ordered to remove trade barriers and tariffs. When poor nations without strong export industries opened their doors to free trade, their domestic markets were inundated with imports, making it all the more difficult for domestic industry to compete. At the same time, the developed world did not follow its own advice in removing tariffs and other barriers to trade. Certain domestic products in the developed world, such as agriculture, continued to receive heavy subsidies, making it even more difficult for less developed countries to compete. Furthermore, trade barriers were typically implemented by developed nations when they were first developing new industries during the Industrial Revolution. If the less developed countries followed the example of the developed world, they would first strengthen their domestic production and then remove barriers to trade only when their own industries were strong enough to handle foreign competition,.

The inattention to *pace* and *sequencing* in implementing these changes in economic policy was responsible for creating much social, economic and political instability.[21] Without stability, development is virtually impossible, as was proven through the years following the fall of the iron curtain. The World Bank and the IMF pursued a policy of economic reform in the former Soviet Union and Eastern Europe known as *Shock Therapy*. The sudden

---

[21] Stiglitz, Joseph E. 2003. *Globalization and Its Discontents*. W. W. Norton & Company.

shift from a central planning to a free market economy did not begin to produce economic growth until almost fifteen years had passed and life had returned to some measure of stability. Rather, these nations first fell into deep recession, with human conditions significantly worse than under the broken communist system. No thought was given to those who had to live during the transition from central planning and closed markets to privatization and liberalization.

2.3.7   Development as a People-Oriented Process:

Since the failures of international development in the 1980s and 1990s, renewed attention has been given to the *process* of development planning as it affects real people over strategies that represent an abstract end-state economic condition. The World Bank has even developed a Participation and Civic Engagement Group to "promote the participation of people and their organizations to influence institutions, policies and processes for equitable and sustainable development."[22] It has discovered that local participation in project selection and design is more likely to be successful. This has been joined to the idea that *democratic* processes produce better projects.

The World Bank has gone as far as developing special grant programs for communities to spend as they see fit. This is a remarkable departure from the development tactics applied by the Bank from the 1950s through the 1990s. While there have been a few cases of grant monies being misspent, the World Bank grant programs have experienced overall success, to the point of being imitated by several countries, such as Thailand. The arguments supporting these programs focus on those factors that made the Marshall Plan such a success:

---

[22] *Participation and Civic Engagement.* The World Bank, November 12, 2008, available at http://www.worldbank.org/participation.

Development Theory and Literature Review

[T]he people in the village know better than anyone else what will make a difference to their lives; they know how the money is spent, and any corruption hurts them directly. Having invested in the planning and execution of a project, they are more likely to feel ownership, a commitment to see it through to success, and therefore more likely to see it receive the funds required to maintain it.[23]

The elements at work in this kind of a development approach are as follow: (1) managed competition among donees, which makes corruption more difficult); (2) human organization and cooperation before funds are granted, making the project more sustainable by building the institutions required to manage the future project into the planning phase; (3) providing grants rather than loans; (4) project planning by those most affected by the project; and (5) solutions that are tailored directly to problems. This approach to development has become synonymous with *building democracy* because it encourages civil society to strengthen itself and to participate in processes that were previously handled exclusively by governments.

However, it should be noted that public participation in development planning is not identical to "democracy" *per se*, which is a political system of both shared power and electoral processes. Rather, the participation approach to planning places people at the center of development by including them in the planning. This is more fundamental to the success of development projects than whether the project takes place in a country with a democratic political system.

The United Nations came to recognize the value of people in measuring development at about the same time as the World Bank. Previous United Nations measures had either directly or indirectly relied on national GDPs as a measure of development. In the early 1990s, the United Nations switched focus and began systematically relying on the Human Development Index (hereinafter, "HDI"),

---

[23] Stiglitz, Joseph E. 2006. *Making Globalization Work*. W. W. Norton & Company.

which includes measures of human life expectancy and educational attainment combined with measures of income. Economic resources are viewed as a means of improving human well-being — not as the goal of development.

Urban Planning in the United States and the United Kingdom has recognized the significance of *processes* in city planning since the 1950s Rational Planning Model was developed. Yet international development theory, recognizing development as an end-state condition rather than as a process, has been slower to catch on. Perhaps the difference in scale between urban planning and international development produced this discrepancy: whereas urban planners are concerned with local economic development, international development is often concerned with growth in national economies, which are intimately tied to the people affected. Whatever the reason for the delay in international development theory, there remains great potential in considering how the lessons learned in urban planning can be applied to international development.

2.4   Public Private Partnerships in International Development

Public Private Partnerships emerged with great popularity in international development under the Washington Consensus mantra of privatization. A PPP is a contract between a public and a private organization. For example, a public bureaucratic agency may enter into a contract with a private janitorial services company to maintain the agency's office facilities. Similarly, a government may sell a nationalized industry to a private sector, which will thereafter handle the provision of some public good to the general population. PPPs are often narrowly conceived to be limited to one of the following types[24]:

---

[24] Table taken from: Sahooly, Anwer. "Public-Private Partnership in the Water Supply and Sanitation Sector: The Experience of the Republic of Yemen." *International Journal of Water Resources Development* (Routledge, June 2003).

Type	Asset ownership	Maintenance	Investment	Duration
Service contract	Public	Public/private	Public	1-2 years
Management contract	Public	Private	Public	3-5 years
Lease	Public	Private	Public	8-15 years
Build, operates, transfer	Private	Private	Private	20-30 years
Concession	Public/private	Private	Private	25-30 years
Divestiture	Private	Private	Private	Indefinite

Just as many of the privatization strategies of the 1980s and 1990s under the IMF's Structural Adjustment Programs were not successful in bringing sustainable economic growth and well-being to the majority of society, so PPPs do not have a solid record of success within the international context. It should be noted that because a PPP is a legally binding agreement, certain legal frameworks must exist in order for the agreement to be enforceable. It is extremely important to have a judicial system independent from any other governmental branches. A private party who signs a contract with a government must have the assurance that if the government does not complete its legal obligations, the private party has legal recourse by which to enforce the terms of the contact. All the same, PPPs remain a favored development tool of the IMF[25] and of the United Nations Development Programme.[26]

---

[25] Gerrard, Michael B. "Public-Private Partnerships." *Finance and Development: A*

General Overview

The World Bank has considered privatization through PPPs to be a central strategy in achieving economic reform in less developed countries in order to promote private investment, create jobs, develop a middle class, shift risk from the public sector to the private sector, and reduce capital flight abroad.[27]

Although PPPs are extremely flexible and can adapt to any terms of negotiation, they are still entrenched in privatization ideology within the international development community. They are viewed as a means of bringing economic reform, as prescribed by the Washington Consensus. However, because of their flexible nature, they nonetheless have the potential to serve as a means of applying development principles that favor civic engagement and participation in development planning. The success of PPPs will depend on their inclusion among the fundamental principles of successful development, which include human organization, managed competition, institution building, the design of solutions to fit problems, and social, political and economic stability.

After all of the theoretical movements that international development has endured since the end of World War II, the future development of the globe still remains uncertain. International development is very difficult to achieve and it takes a long time. Stories of failed policies are more prevalent than those of successful policies. Despite this great challenge, there remains a small hope that the international development community has moved beyond over-simplistic models and is beginning to embrace the complexity of each individual as a contributor to the success or failure of his or her nation in the new era of globalization.

Quarterly Magazine of the IMF (International Monetary Fund, Sept. 2001).

[26] *Special Unit for South-South Cooperation.* United Nations Development Programme, November 12., 2008, available at http://www.ncppp.org/undp/index.html. (showing that PPPs are utilized as a tool for reaching development objectives by the Special Unit for South-South Cooperation of the United Nations Development Programme).

[27] Guislain, Pierre. *The Privatization Challenge: A Strategic, Legal, and Institutional Analysis of International Experience* (World Bank, 1997), p. 18-19.

Development Theory and Literature Review

Chapter 3.

"FREEDOM" AND "DEVELOPMENT"

"A state that denies itself open, democratic processes and institutions will thereby impede the development and progress of its people, denying them the chance to interact fully with the wider world."
Kofi Annan[28]

"Freedom" and "development" are two words that are often thrown together in international development circles. Libertarian organizations that promote economic freedom as the key to development, such as the Cato Institute, the Institute for Humane Studies, and the Fraser Institute, as well as the World Trade Organization, the Bretton Woods Institutions, several branches of the United Nations, and countless think tanks and universities around the globe have linked policies that promote freedom with increased development. Even the U.S. Agency for International Development (USAID), an independent federal agency that receives overall foreign policy guidelines from the Secretary of State, has a specific mission to "[expand] democracy and free markets while improving the lives of the citizens of the developing world."[29]

If this vast array of organizations assumes a relationship between "freedom" and "development," then what is that

---

[28] Annan, Kofi. April 12, 2000. "Secretary-General, in Havana on Eve of First 'Group of 77' Summit Meeting, Evokes Promises and Pitfalls of Globalization" in UN Press Release. SG/SM/7357.
[29] USAID: About USAID. U.S. Agency for International Development, Nov. 1, 2008, available at http://www.usaid.gov/about_usaid/.

relationship? It is this question that has prompted this author to conduct an analysis of over 140 nations to test whether such a relationship exists and, if so, to determine the nature of that relationship. Before this can be undertaken, however, it is important to define development and to parse between the uses of the word "freedom," distinguishing between references to democracy and references to human rights.

3.1 Development: Increasing Human Well-Being

In the most generic terms, development can be understood as the process of bringing some object into a more advanced state. The traditional umbrella of international development has included economic, technological, and human development, as well as urban and infrastructure development. Each of these areas of development can be measured and is used to rank nations comparatively against each other for their overall state of advancement. In my analysis, however, the measure of a developed society will be restricted to the most fundamental unit: human beings, since, after all, "[p]eople are the real wealth of nations."[30]

The UNDP has developed the Human Development Index ("HDI"), which ranks nations according to their overall human development score. The HDI score is a simple measurement of several factors, including the life expectancy, educational attainment, and income levels of the general population. "The most basic capabilities for human development are to lead long and healthy lives, to be knowledgeable, to have access to the resources needed for a decent standard of living and to be able to participate in the life of the community."[31] In this context, monetary wealth is simply a means for improving the well-being of the population. It is this improvement in human well-being that will serve as the definition of "development," as measured by UNDP's HDI score,

---

[30] *The Human Development Concept.* United Nations Development Programme, Nov. 1, 2008, available at http://hdr.undp.org/en/humandev/
[31] *Ibid.*

"Freedom" and "Development"

to be used in examining the relationship between "freedom" and "development."

3.2   Freedom: Democracy and Human Rights

"Freedom" in the international development literature is generally intended to mean democratization, protection of human rights or free access to markets. Because the freedom to engage in business—*i.e.*, to access markets—falls under the larger subject of human rights protections, my analysis will only examine the significance of democracy and human rights as measures of freedom in effecting development.

Democracy and human rights are fundamentally different concepts. Whereas human rights are moral entitlements recognized by societies, democracy is a political system of shared power and electoral processes. Human rights include political rights and civil liberties, such as equality before the law, the right to engage in political activity, freedom of expression, the right to work, and the right to hold private property. The United Nations is perhaps the best modern source for defining human rights, considering it published the 1948 Universal Declaration of Human Rights, the first article of which lays the foundation for all subsequent rights in stating that "[a]ll human beings are born free and equal in dignity and rights…"[32]

Measuring the level of human rights in a nation is a matter of comparing that nation's laws protecting individuals and the enforcement of these laws against the moral entitlements of all human beings. Freedom House, a non-profit non-partisan organization founded in 1941 for the promotion of freedom and democracy around the world, conducts an annual survey of over 190 nations to assess their level of political rights and civil liberties, and thereby assess their overall measure of freedom.[33] The scores

---

[32] *Universal Declaration of Human Rights*. United Nations, Nov. 1, 2008, available at http://www.un.org/Overview/rights.html.
[33] Freedom in the World. Freedom House, Nov. 1, 2008, available at

for political rights and civil liberties for their latest survey were taken from seven subcategories drawn from the Universal Declaration of Human Rights, which include the individual's right to:

(1)   "Participate freely in the political process;
(2)   Vote freely in legitimate elections;
(3)   Have representatives that are accountable to them;
(4)   Exercise freedoms of expression and belief;
(5)   Be able to freely assemble and associate;
(6)   Have access to an established and equitable system of rule of law;
(7)   Have social and economic freedoms, including equal access to economic opportunities and the right to hold private property."[34]

The separate scores for political rights and civil liberties for each nation per year are key measurements for determining the relationship between freedom and development.

While political rights and civil liberties are entitlements of independent choice, democracy is a political system built on strong civil society. Being an ancient concept, there have been many definitions of democracy throughout history. "According to Aristotle, the rule of the one and the rule of the many represent the two extremes of a continuum from autocracy to democracy."[35] The two significant components of modern democratic systems are competition among political parties and free and fair elections. If there is only one political party and one candidate on the ballot, then elections are virtually meaningless. If there are multiple parties competing for power, but only a select group of elites are

---

http://www.freedomhouse.org/.

[34] *Ibid.*

[35] Vanhanen, Tatu. 2000. *Polyarchy Dataset Manuscript.* International Peace Research Institute, Oslo. Available at http://www.prio.no/CSCW/Datasets/Governance/Vanhanens-index-of-democracy/Polyarchy-Dataset-Manuscript/.

permitted to vote, then to call the system democratic is untrue. Democracy is "a political system in which ideologically and socially different groups are legally entitled to compete for political power and in which institutional power holders are elected by the people and are responsible to the people."[36] In a study conducted by Professor Emeritus Tatu Vanhanen called the Polyarchy Dataset, every nation was given a score for each year for its measure of competition among political parties, and for the measure of public participation in the electoral process. While these two measures are equally important to a complete democratic system, the significance of each measure has been treated separately in examining the relationship between freedom and development. This is simply to determine if one is more significant than the other in effecting development.

3.3   Effecting Development

What is the relationship between freedom and democracy? Returning to this question, this author conducted a global analysis covering twenty five years of data to explore the possibility of a causal relationship between freedom and development. The purpose of the analysis was to substantiate the assumption that freedom leads to development with evidence collected at the global scale. If the goal of international development is to reach across national boundaries and improve the lives of citizens in the developing world, then any assumptions driving international development decisions should be rooted in the global context. By testing assumptions, the analysis clarifies the lens through which the specific case studies examined in the next chapter are harvested for "keys" to their success or failure. The case studies become learning lessons in lieu of wild cards when they can be understood as culturally contextual applications of trends that hold true in the global context.

---

[36] *Ibid.*

General Overview

The first part of the study was to collect data that represents measures of human development and freedom, which correspond to the United Nations Development Programme's HDI values, Tatu Vanhanen's Polyarchy Dataset, and Freedom House's Freedom Score. It should be noted that a lower Freedom Score corresponds to a higher level of freedom. Also, the dataset and the analyses are both available in Appendix A.

The second step towards analyzing the data was to form a hypothesis against which to check the data. My first hypothesis was that those nations which become freer over a period of five years would most likely become more developed over the same five year period. This assumption is subsequently referred to as "The Freedom Hypothesis." As a means of examining this assumption, the present author created a scatter graph for five year periods of time (for example, 1975-1980; 1980-1985, etc.) which graphically plotted the amount of change in the HDI score and the amount of change in one of the freedom measures for each country from a point 0,0. If a nation's data supported the Freedom Hypothesis, then it would show that it had both increased in human development and increased in freedom over the same five year period of time (meaning, it would show up as a plot point in the quadrant that reflect gains in HDI values *and* freedom measures). If it did not support the hypothesis, then that would also be reflected in the scatter graph. If a nation increased in a freedom score but did not change their HDI value, or if the inverse was true, then this was considered as evidence that was neutral to the hypothesis.

After examining the data, it was determined that there is no evidence to support the Freedom Hypothesis. While some nations might become freer while also increasing their HDI values, it is apparent that other unknown factors make a more significant contribution to a change in HDI scores than the freedom measures that were analyzed in this study.

34

"Freedom" and "Development"

After the data was plotted on individual scatter graphs, the present author proposed a second hypothesis. It appeared that the majority of nations that experienced increases in their HDI values over five years had a relatively low *change* in their freedom level, whether positive or negative. This author identified this low level of change in freedom as representing *stability*. The Stability Hypothesis subsequently emerged as assuming that those nations with stable levels of freedom over five years were more likely to increase their HDI value over the same five year period. Nations were counted as "stable" if they had only changed a little in the level of freedom (that is, their competition or participation scores varied by less than ten, and their political rights and civil liberties scores varied by less than one). The results demonstrated that there is a relationship between stability and human development.

Surprisingly, the results yielded little to no evidence that improving democracy and human rights protections result in the improvement of human development. Instead, the analysis demonstrated that keeping human rights protections and democracy levels steady, whether they remain the same or experience small incremental changes, is more likely to produce improvements in human development levels. While it acknowledged that a freer society is better for people, transitions towards freedom should be made in baby steps. Maintaining stability is crucial to success in increasing development.

Stable governments provide a context for sustainable development. Sustainability — the ability to maintain something indefinitely — requires a measure of certainty and confidence that the resources needed for maintenance will remain available. The availability of resources from an investor has much to do with the investor's perception of risk, as their willingness to invest increases with the certainty that the environment will not change for the worse. An "investor" could be an individual investing in their own education or a foreign bank investing in private businesses. Whether large investor or small, stability is crucial to reducing perceived risk and to maintaining sustainable gains in human development. Even Joseph Stiglitz, a Nobel prize-winning economist, has recognized that "[democracy] is neither a necessary nor a sufficient condition for successful development... [though he] would argue that it helps achieve sustainable development... [His] view is that successful development requires infrastructure, social and political stability and full employment."[37]

3.4   Promoting Democracy and Human Rights

If democracy and human rights are not significant contributors to development, then why is the United States foreign policy to build civil society and to "[expand] democracy and free markets while improving the lives of the citizens of the developing world"?[38] Why do so many organizations insist that there is a link between freedom and development? Why does UNDP state that "[human] development and human rights are mutually reinforcing"?[39] The answer to these questions relates to stability and peace.

The interests of the American people and of the international community are served when a state of security and stability prevails. United States foreign policy has been to reinforce stability *through* democracy and free markets from the close of World War II. It was the conviction of Cordell Hull, the Secretary of State under President Franklin Roosevelt, that both world wars had originated with the strict trade barriers that existed between the European nations and their rivals' colonies.[40] The goal of the Marshall Plan was to restructure an economic interdependence

---

[37] Vogler, Justin. "Democratising globalisation: Joseph Stiglitz interviewed." *Open Democracy: Free Thinking for the World* (September 2006). Available at http://www.opendemocracy.net/globalization-vision_reflections/stiglitz_3931.jsp.

[38] USAID: About USAID. U.S. Agency for International Development, Nov. 1, 2008, available at http://www.usaid.gov/about_usaid/.

[39] *The Human Development Concept*. United Nations Development Programme, Nov. 1, 2008, available at http://hdr.undp.org/en/humandev/

[40] Hull, Cordell (1948). *The Memoirs of Cordell Hull*. New York: Macmillan.

between the European nations as had never previously existed, making war between them impossible. The European Union grew out of this economic restructuring. Open markets work to build bridges across the network of nations While not always effective, these bridges also provide the means of enforcing economic sanctions on nations who threaten global stability.

Similarly, truly democratic systems also contribute to stability in the world because, in a democratic system with a strong civil society, power is shared among many. This is not to say that all democracies have a broad power base among the public. Many democracies, unfortunately, continue to concentrate power in the hands of a few. Under these conditions, it only takes the removal of a few individuals to place a great vacuum of power on the open market for sale. The ease with which power can be shifted from one group to another contributes to the volatility of governments. When the power base is broadly spread across the population, as in a democratic system as defined by Aristotle, it creates the foundation for stability in government.

Stability and world peace are clearly significant favors in increasing human development. As war and destruction are suspended, and governments are stable, the environment is more conducive to investment and development. International development agencies will continue to promote democratization and human rights protections as a key to development. However, a direct relationship between freedom and development does not exist. Yet, as these agencies promote freedom, any intended or unintended contribution to stability will create the environment for greater human development.

3.5   Freedom and Public Private Partnerships

PPPs provide an opportunity for creative responses to development demands. Although stability is significant to increasing development, managed competition to reduce corruption, human organization, institution building, and the design of solutions to fit the problem are also very important to consider. The idea that negotiations between the public and private sector can then be translated into a contractual agreement through a PPP first depends upon the ability of fair negotiations between parties. PPPs create an open market between the public and private sector where competing ideas from both sectors can simultaneously create opportunities for risk sharing and private ownership in meeting social and economic challenges while empowering citizens with access to public resources.

Previously defined as a contract between a public organization and a private organization, not all PPPs have been a means of garnering private participation in development planning. However, the potential to use PPPs in creating sustainable development remains. How this potential may become realized in a PPP structure is explored in the following chapter.

Chapter 4.

PUBLIC PRIVATE PARTNERSHIP CASE STUDIES

Public Private Partnerships are a unique structure by which the public and private sectors can unite in serving a local or national community. As with most contractual agreements, the legally binding terms of the PPP are preceded by negotiations. It is during the negotiation phase of a PPP that public participation and civic engagement can play a strong role in determining the future success of the PPP. The flexibility of PPPs also allows for them to become the means of implementing broader principles that strengthen development, such as managed competition to reduce corruption, human organization and coordination for sustainable development, maintaining economic, social and political stability, solutions designed to fit specific problems, and attention to people as most important in any development strategy.

The following case studies serve as examples of partnerships between public and private organizations. These cases will be studied for how well they implemented the principles that have emerged throughout this thesis as the most significant to successful development policy and implementation. Each case will be compared against the previously identified principles for successful development as a means of testing whether these principles can truly be applied successfully across a broad range of contexts. For this reason, this set of cases represents a diverse group of circumstances and time periods.

The cases that will be examined are: (1) the World Bank's implementation of PPPs in the water sector in Yemen from the late 1990s to the present; (2) community organization and urban revitalization in Boston, Massachusetts, from the mid 1980s to the present; and (3) regional community and economic development in

Emilia Romagna, Italy, from the 1940s to the present, with specific emphasis on how small businesses engage in global competition.

The case in Yemen was chosen because it represents a current example of how the international development community has been applying PPPs to bring development to a less developed country. In this case, it is yet to be determined whether these strategies will be successful. However, the case represents an opportunity to explore the current procedures surrounding PPP implementation in less developed countries and whether there are opportunities for public participation in that process.

The second case will examine the Boston, Massachusetts Dudley Street Neighborhood, which established a community organization and eventually developed a very unique partnership with the Boston city government. This case was chosen because it represents a completely different context than is usually treated in international development literature. However, if the principles that lead to successful development are true in small villages in India, they ought to be true in urban America as well. This case is an opportunity to test that assumption.

The third case will examine the Emilia Romagna region of Italy, which has a history of cooperatives dating back to the 1860s. What is distinctive about these cooperatives is the partnership that has developed between the local government and the cooperatives since the 1940s. The region is one of the most successful examples of transformation from a poor rural agricultural community into one of the wealthiest regions in Europe with a diversified economy and a median income that is fifty percent higher than the national average. Besides its history of success, this case was chosen because Italy has been compared to many less developed countries in that it has very strong family networks and it has had many challenges with corruption. More specifically, this region is characterized by medium and small business (as opposed to the large corporations of the United States) which is a challenge that many less developed countries face as well when competing in the global market. This select aspect of the Emilia Romagna case will be studied for how and if it reflects the principles of successful development identified earlier.

After a brief historical narrative, each case will be studied for whether principles of sustainable development were applied, namely: solutions that fit problems, managed competition, human organization, institution building and stability. Each case will then be studied for what the partnership between the public and private sector was, by what process the partnership was established, and for how the partnership implemented or did not implement good development principles. The goal of this study is to further explore the potential for PPPs to build sustainable development through public participation and time-tested development principles.

4.1 Cooperative Success and the Role of Local Government

4.1.1 Overview

Emilia Romagna is a region in north-central Italy with a long history of cooperatives that date back as early as the 1860s. By the 1920s, there were 3,600 consumer cooperatives and 2,700 production cooperatives in the region. However, when the Fascist Party took control of all cooperatives in 1926, the two decades that insured were marked by struggle and by the end of World War II, the region was in economic ruin.[41]

Although Emilia Romagna was once one of the poorest of the industrialized regions of Italy, today, it has a population of around 3.9 million, which is seven percent of the population of Italy, yet it accounts for nine percent of the Italian GDP, twelve percent of Italian export, and thirty percent of Italy's patents. Unemployment is around three percent and it also boasts a median income that is fifty percent higher than the national average.[42]

---

[41] Thompson, David J. 2003. *Italy's Emilia Romagna: Clustering Co-op Development.* Cooperative Grocer: For Retailers and Cooperators. No. 109.
[42] Logue, John. 2006 *Economics and Cooperation: The Emilia Romagna Model.* OurBiz

General Overview

Since the end of World War II, Emilia Romagna has continuous elected left-wing governing officials. While the CIA was pouring money into the industrial left-wing regions of Italy in the heat of the Cold War, the Emilia Romagna region was too small to be noticed. It was during this time that the local government stepped up to support the regions small businesses as a strategy for economic development.

The businesses in the Emilia Romagna region are still very small today, with one firm for every nine people, many of which are family owned. While cooperatives employ only ten percent of the workforce, they generate about thirty percent of the regional GDP. The success of the region has been a direct result of the government's role in promoting small businesses.

To briefly review the legal structure of Italy's employee-owned cooperatives, the Basevi Law of 1947 established the rules and tax structures that would govern cooperatives.[43] Cooperatives are allowed to make tax free contributes into an "indivisible reserve" (about a forty percent savings in taxes) for reinvestment into the cooperative. However, should the cooperative dissolve, the law requires the reserves transfer to anther cooperative or cooperative federation rather than be distributed among the members.

Employee cooperative are owned completely by their members and are operated by an elected board. Membership fees can range anywhere from six months of service and a $3,000 membership fee to five years of service and an $112,000 membership fee. The tax benefits governing employee cooperatives is the same for firms with both a large and a small percentage of employee members. The percentage of employees who are members varies across cooperative firms in Emilia Romagna, where one-hundred percent of employees are members in some firms, and only ten percent of employees are members in others. The members

---

International. December 10, 2006.
[43] *Ibid.*

receive their returns in annual interest payments on their membership fees and in patronage dividends. Interest payments are typically around nine percent and patronage dividends can range anywhere from the equivalent of one to four months salary at the cooperative.

Small businesses were promoted by the regional government particularly in the 1970s and 1980s through the creation of industrial sector service centers. In 1974, the Regional Board for Economic Development was established with the main objective of providing real services through centers to the small businesses of Emilia Romagna.[44] The idea was to achieve economies of scale among small business in a particular sector by clustering them together and providing services in research and development, purchasing, education and training, workplace safety, technology transfer, marketing and distribution, exporting and all kinds of services that a small business would typically have to pay special consultants to do. The goal of these agencies was to provide small businesses with low-cost high-quality services that a large business would typically conduct in house.

The industrial sector service centers have also encouraged "flexible manufacturing," in which small businesses in the same industry partner together in joint bids for large contracts. For example, the region produces parts for companies such as Ferrari, Lamborghini, Maserati and Ducati all through networks of small businesses.[45] In addition to partnering with the cooperatives, the service centers also partner with credit and financial institutions, entrepreneurial associations and the Chamber of Commerce.

Since the 1970s and 1980s, many cooperatives have joined umbrella cooperative federations, the three largest of which are the left-wing Legacoop, the Catholic Confcooperative, and a smaller

---

[44] Danson, Michael and Geoff Whittam. 1999. *Regional Governance, Institutions and Development*. Regional Research Institute, West Virginia Univeristy.
[45] Logue, John. 2006 *Economics and Cooperation: The Emilia Romagna Model*. OurBiz International. December 10, 2006.

Republican/Social Democratic group. These cooperative federations are like cooperatives for cooperatives. They provide many of the same services that the government-run service centers provide in addition to such services as tax preparation, accounting, payroll and legal services; training and development; occupational health and safety consulting; collective bargaining; waste disposal; and lending and equity investment from its development fund. Member cooperatives pay fees to the cooperative federations in order to participate in the benefits offered, which have included such special projects as daycare centers for members and restaurants.

Not only has the collaboration between cooperatives led to the success of the region, but the support of the local government to small businesses through small service contracts has created an extremely high-value and flexible production system. Small businesses are able to compete in the global market unlike most other regions of the globe characterized by small businesses. The success of Emilia Romagna is a potential model for less developed countries to learn from.

4.1.2 *Principles for Successful Development*

Emilia Romagna faced a challenge in regional economic development with an abundance of businesses too small to take advantage of economies of scale and compete fairly against big businesses from other regions in Italy. The creation of industrial sector service centers brought small businesses within the same sector together, allowing them retain their individual identity while providing the organizational framework for them to receive the same benefits as large corporations. The alliances between small businesses in bidding on large contracts were made possible through the government service centers. The flexibility in this type of production system allows small businesses to compete both globally and locally.

Public Private Partnership Case Studies

The government service centers also set a pattern for cooperatives to coordinate among themselves through cooperative federations. These federations have infinitely broadened small businesses' access to special services, further diversifying the regional economy.

Additionally, cooperatives are seen as a source of economic stability for the region. Because the cooperatives are member-owned, and the "indivisible reserves" are kept within the cooperative structure, the long-term investment of cooperatives in themselves allows cooperatives to weather the waves of market fluctuation.

4.1.3   Public Private Partnership

The thought of a PPP typically conjures up an image of the private sector providing a contracted service to the public sector. The case in Emilia Romagna does not fit this paradigm. Rather, the public sector provided services for a fee to small private businesses and cooperatives. The partnership in this case was initiated by the regional government in Emilia Romagna. Considering the government provided services for sale in the market, they must have had some understanding of what the demand for such services was. Ultimately, the partnerships gave the smaller businesses equal access to markets as larger businesses, and the economic growth of the entire region expanded with the success of the small cooperatives and businesses.

4.2   Community Organizing

4.2.1   Overview

The Dudley Street Neighborhood, located in Roxbury, Massachusetts, has been hailed as a national model of successful urban revitalization. Thriving small businesses and great food characterize this neighborhood of diverse ethnic backgrounds just outside of downtown Boston. Twenty five years ago, however, the streets depicted a different picture. In the 1980s, the Dudley Street (hereinafter, "DS") neighborhood was suffering from white flight, arson fires set by landlords to collect insurance, disinvestment from banks and neglect.[46] With approximately one third of the land burnt out and vacant, it was the image of urban blight.

About ten years earlier, in 1971, Mabel Louise Riley, an heiress to a successful machine company, died at age eighty-eight, and left a large fortune in trust for public and charitable uses.[47] The Mabel Louise Riley Foundation (hereinafter, "Riley Foundation") was formed in 1972 and immediately became an active philanthropic agency in the Boston area.

In 1984, a group from the Riley Foundation toured the DS neighborhood and decided that revitalizing the neighborhood was the kind of project that fit with its mission. A number of community organizations already existed in the DS area. The Riley Foundation brought the leaders of these organizations together in a series of meetings which transformed into the "Dudley Advisor Group." The Riley Foundation was known as a big donor and purposefully took a back seat, letting those with first hand knowledge of the neighborhood problems run the meetings and propose solutions. The most important decision that the group made after one month of meetings was to form an organization, namely, the Dudley Street Neighborhood Initiative (hereinafter, "DSNI").[48]

Over the next four years, the Riley Foundation poured nearly $2 million into the DSNI. The organization was officially incorporated in 1985 as a 501 (c)(3) nonprofit organization. While it was originally thought that the organization would act as an

---

[46] Barros, John. 2001. "Youth Leadership Development: A Space, a Voice and Some Power." The Nonprofit Quarterly, Vol. 8, Issue 4.

[47] Mabel Louise Riley Foundation, November 16, 2008, available at http://www.rileyfoundation.com.

[48] Medoff, Peter, and Holly Sklar. *Streets of Hope: The Fall and Rise of an Urban Neighborhood.* Published by Peter Medoff and Holly Sklar, 1994.

umbrella for the existing community organization in the neighborhood to coordinate efforts, it became apparent at the first community meeting that the residents wanted control. They were not satisfied to allow the community organizations to represent them. The bylaws were subsequently written to ensure that resident members always retained a 51 percent majority. A fair representation of all ethnic groups in the neighborhood was also integral to how the bylaws structured the governing board. Other bylaw provisions permitted the DSNI to engage in partnerships, joint ventures, and other enterprises so long as it accomplished the mission of the initiative.[49]

In the first year after a board was elected, in 1986, the newly hired staff organized a neighborhood campaign to clean up all the vacant lots which had become illegal dumping grounds. The neighborhood had approximately 5,500 residents at that time, with over one third under the age of eighteen. The following year, the DSNI put out a request for proposals for consultant services to help create a master plan for the neighborhood. DAC International, an African-American consulting firm based in Washington DC, was hired to create a "Dudley Street Neighborhood Comprehensive Revitalization Plan," which was subsequently adopted by the Boston Redevelopment Authority. DAC was selected by the DSNI committee over two local consulting firms because they were specifically committed to maximizing resident participation in the planning process.

After surveys, community meetings, demographic studies, and charrettes (design workshops), a comprehensive plan which reflected the community's values emerged. The next step for DSNI was to create an implementation strategy. Part of the comprehensive revitalization plan was to bring new housing development back to the neighborhood. However, they soon realized that the multitude of vacant lots were actually a puzzle of

---

[49] The Dudley Street Neighborhood Initiative, November 16, 2008, available at http://www.dsni.org.

private property and city-owned property. In order to the sort through the legalities of redeveloping abandoned land, the DSNI promptly hired a law firm, Rackemann, Sawyer and Brewster, to scope the possibility of using eminent domain to acquire the property. The firm responded with two options: eminent domain powers were available to the Boston Redevelopment Authority, and to private corporations who applied for Chapter 121A Urban Redevelopment Corporation status under the Massachusetts General Law. The DSNI took the latter option in 1988 and created Dudley Neighbors, Inc., then subsequently applied and was granted eminent domain authority through the provisions of Chapter 121A.[50]

The Chapter 121A Urban Revitalization Corporation is a means by which the private sector can organize and propose a revitalization project in an area classified as "blighted," "decadent" or "sub-standard" in exchange for tax incentives.[51] The applicants are required to submit a proposal to the local housing authority (the Boston Redevelopment Authority in the case of DSNI) for a project which may include limited eminent domain authority for the applicant. Once the project is approved, then the applicant submits to the state for incorporation as either a non-profit charitable corporation, a for-profit business corporation, or a for-profit cooperative business corporation. In 1966, the Massachusetts state legislature had voted to extend the provisions of the Chapter 121A to allow charitable corporations to "undertake or acquire or carry on urban redevelopment projects."[52] Non-profit organizations that are granted Chapter 121A Urban Revitalization Corporation

---

[50] Medoff, Peter, and Holly Sklar. *Streets of Hope: The Fall and Rise of an Urban Neighborhood.* Published by Peter Medoff and Holly Sklar, 1994.

[51] Urban Revitalization Corporations, Chapter 121A, General Law of Massachusetts. November 16, 2008, available at http://www.mass.gov/legis/laws/mgl/gl-121a-toc.htm.

[52] Acts of 1966, State Library of Massachusetts, November 16, 2008, available at http://archives.lib.state.ma.us/actsResolves/1966/1966acts0421.pdf.

status are only allowed to reinvest profits in subsequent revitalization projects.

Dudley Neighbors, Inc. is structured as a Community Land Trust (hereinafter, "CLT"), which is a concept that developed in the 1960s. The CLT acquires and holds land which it leases to homeowners, usually for ninety-nine years. The lease is renewable and can be transferred to children. Homeowners can sell their house, but not the land. When they sell their house, the lease on the land requires the home to be either sold back to the CLT or to another low-income household for an affordable price.[53] Many neighborhoods similar to DS were experiencing gentrification and displacement of their low-income residents as a result of revitalization development projects. The CLT structure was crucial to preserving affordable housing in the DS neighborhood and keeping the residents in their homes. Because Dudley Neighbors, Inc. is directed by the community-led DSNI, residents had a direct means of controlling the development process.

Since 1988, DSNI has continued to initiate successful programs for its members, who have been instrumental in the creation of gardens, parks, playgrounds, new homes, schools, community centers and a Town Common. They have received numerous awards and continue to be a model for other neighborhoods facing similar challenges.

4.2.2 Principles for Successful Development

Vacant land in the DS neighborhood was originally considered a liability. However, when land was eventually perceived as a community asset, it transformed the strategy for revitalization, placing the asset firmly into the hands of the residents through the Community Land Trust. This provided protection for residents against capital seeking undervalued land

---

[53] *Community Land Trust Model.* Institute for Community Economics, November 16, 1008, available at http://www.iceclt.org/clt/cltmodel.html.

for redevelopment, which would have resulted in increased property values and eventual displacement of the low-income community. The solution to collect vacant land through eminent domain and hold it in trust fit the problem that undervalued vacant land tempting investors would have created for the community.

The early role that the Riley Foundation played in bringing the leaders of the non-profit community organizations together was remarkable in that it proposed funding a neighborhood initiative, but first required the community organizations to coordinate among themselves. Rather than funding each group individually, the donor first required the groups to participate in creating the organization that would become the vehicle for neighborhood-wide change before funding the project. The existing competition among ethnic community organizations for donor funds had to be tabled in the Dudley Advisory Group discussions about what would improve the neighborhood. Even in the governing structure of the DSNI, a delicate balance of power had to be created to the satisfaction of all ethnic groups to assure residence of their representation on the board of directors. The Riley Foundation set the stage for managed competition among all community members, ensuring transparency and efficiency with donor monies, and a commitment to promote programs that benefit all.

The initiative of the Dudley Advisory Group in proposing an umbrella community organization is what first prompted a series of community meetings that in turn opened the door for residents to participate and demand more control over the organizations' decision-making procedures. The level of human organization that spawned from the early community meetings far surpassed anything that the original Dudley Advisory Group had ever imagined. Although this group of organized citizens still relied heavily on contracted consultants, the final decisions were made by the residents through the board of directors and the voting members. The DSNI became the institution that sustained the revitalization programs and brought transformation to the neighborhood with people at the center of their work. The DS neighborhood implemented principles of development that brought sustained success for their community.

4.2.3 Public Private Partnership

The first partnership in the Dudley Street case was between the residents of the neighborhood. Once the neighborhood had become organized through the DSNI, they were positioned to partner with the City of Boston, through the Boston Redevelopment Authority, in creating a Chapter 121A Corporation. Dudley Neighbors, Inc.'s eminent domain authority was not the result of the Boston Redevelopment Authority deciding to dole out powers typically reserved for public agencies. Rather, it was because the neighborhood had organized themselves into a corporation. This corporation was then able to create another corporation for urban redevelopment according to Massachusetts state law. The right for a private corporation to assume eminent domain authority was granted under the provisions of the Massachusetts law back in the Act of 1960. The PPP between the DSNI and the City of Boston was simply a matter of acquiring approval from the Boston Redevelopment Authority for Dudley Neighbors, Inc.'s proposed project, which subsequently granted them Chapter 121A Urban Redevelopment Corporation status.

The PPP that established Dudley Neighbors, Inc. was the result of the comprehensive master plan that DAC International had created with lots of community participation. Being that the directors of Dudley Neighbors, Inc. are the residents of the neighborhood, the partnership represents the ultimate form of citizen empowerment, and the results can be widely seen in the vibrant DS neighborhood today.

PART 2.
Studies within the Middle Eastern Context

Chapter 5.

YEMEN: THE WORLD BANK'S PPP INITIATIVES
IN THE WATER SECTOR

5.1   Overview

It is widely recognized that the water situation in Yemen borders on crisis. Not only is water being pumped out of the ground at an estimated 138 percent of the annual renewal rate, but both urban and rural water delivery and sanitation are below international standards.[54] Near the capital city of Sana'a, the water basin is currently experiencing an overdraft of 150 percent, with the water table dropping by seven meters per year.[55] Ta'iz, the third largest city in Yemen, also has extreme water shortages. Yemen has engaged multiple strategies for tackling the pending water crisis, including restructuring the urban water sector with the goal of privatization through PPPs. After nearly a decade of reform in the water sector, a PPP was finally signed in Ta'iz in 2006, though not in Sana'a.

Yemen is one of the world's least developed nations. In 2004, it ranked 149 out of 175 countries on the Human Development Index. It has an economic growth rate of 3.461 percent, but a population growth rate of 6.7 percent. With an unemployment rate of 35 percent and inflation at a stifling 20.8 percent, one in five

---

[54] *Yemen Country Profile: Natural Resources.* United Nations Development Programme, Yemen, 30 Oct. 2007, available at http://www.undp.org.ye/resources.php.
[55] Sahooly, Anwer. "Public-Private Partnership in the Water Supply and Sanitation Sector: The Experience of the Republic of Yemen." *International Journal of Water Resources Development* (Routledge, June 2003).

people are malnourished.[56] Part of the challenge in raising the development level in Yemen is that its population is mostly rural, and is therefore spread-out geographically. Another challenge that faces Yemen is the production and consumption of qat, an addictive stimulant grown domestically. It is estimated that 90 percent of all water consumption in Yemen is by the agriculture sector. While the plant is a productive cash crop for farmers, it requires a lot of water to grow, exacerbating the water shortage in the country. Additionally, up to three quarters of the adult population spend one-quarter to one-third of their income on qat. People spend several hours each afternoon sitting together chewing the leaves of the qat plant.[57] It is difficult to get farmers to switch to food crops when qat receives a higher price in the market.

As of 2002, the domestic water service covered about only forty percent of the urban population and thirty percent of the rural population.[58] The rest of the population either collected water from private wells or mosques or purchased water from trucks that brought it from the rural areas into the city. The management of water consumption and water rights has remained one of the largest challenges in meeting the pending crisis in Yemen. In some regions, water has been considered a free public resource. In other areas, rights to water have been negotiated between tribes over centuries. Up until 2004, there were no restrictions or permits required for the construction of private wells. However, with the overdraft of groundwater by farmers, water resource management

---

[56]   *Yemen.*   World   Bank,   November   14,   2008,   available   at http://web.worldbank.org/WBSITE/ EXTERNAL/COUNTRIES/MENAEXT/YEMENEXTN/0,,menuPK:310170~page PK:141159~piPK:141110~theSitePK:310165,00.html.

[57] Milich, Lenard and Mohammed Al-Sabbry. 1995. *The "Rational Peasant" vs Sustainable Livelihoods: The Case of Qat in Yemen.* The University of Arizona.

[58] Sahooly, Anwer. "Public-Private Partnership in the Water Supply and Sanitation Sector: The Experience of the Republic of Yemen." *International Journal of Water Resources Development* (Routledge, June 2003).

has become an imperative for the greater good of the public. The track record of urban water management has not been very good either. For example, in 1999, in Sana'a, over fifty percent of domestic water consumption was unaccounted for and revenue for this water was uncollected.[59]

The World Bank, which has been involved in Yemen since the 1970s, has continued to consult the fledgling government after unification in 1990, especially during the process of liberalization and reform in the 1990s, when it provided expert consultation via the International Development Association. Although the World Bank had recognized that groundwater in Yemen was being depleted as early as 1968, it was not until 1992 that the Bank made its first attempt to address water as a diminishing resource requiring management. The Land and Water Conservation Project began in 1992 and ended in 2000. The goal was to improve irrigation technology in rural Yemen. Overall, the project was successful, as the Yemeni government has continued the program after the World Bank completed their involvement. [60]

In 1995, as the water crisis in Yemen moved to the forefront of the international donor community's agenda, the Multi Donor Group for Yemen Water was formed with the United Nations Development Programme, the Netherlands, and the World Bank as principle members.[61] It was agreed that a coordinated approach to the water problem would produce the best results without duplicating efforts. That same year, the government of Yemen passed a decree to create the National Water and Sanitation Authority (hereinafter, "NWSA").[62] After years of trying to work with the former dispersed and uncoordinated High Water Council,

---

[59] *Ibid.*

[60] *Project Performance Assessment Report: Yemen.* World Bank, Feb. 2006, Report No. 35004.

[61] Dervis, Kemal et. al. Yemen - *Toward a Water Strategy: An Agenda for Action* (World Bank, Aug. 1997).

[62] *Ibid.*

the new NWSA consolidated water resource management and planning into a single agency for all of Yemen.

Soon thereafter, the World Bank initiated another major project in the water sector. The city of Ta'iz was experiencing extreme water shortages in 1996. Piped water was only available every forty days. When the city water runs out in Yemen, people line up outside of mosques to fetch water to carry home for basic cooking and cleaning needs. Time spent fetching water is time taken away from doing other more productive things, such as attending school. The World Bank's Ta'iz Water Supply Pilot Project was a plan to drill wells in the surrounding rural farms, and then pipe the water into the city of Ta'iz. The farmers were compensated for their loss of groundwater. [63] The projected ended in 2001 and was considered unsuccessful because it was not a sustainable solution to the water shortage.

Between the creation of the NWSA in 1995 and 1997, the German Development Corporation, *Deutsche Gesellschaft für Technische Zusammenarbeit* (hereinafter, "GTZ"), provided consultant services to the Ministry of Electricity and Water regarding continued reforms of the new NWSA structure. [64] By November, 1997, the government of Yemen passed the Cabinet Resolution 237, which outlined the new structure for the NWSA and divided Yemen into fourteen water management districts. [65]

In August 1997, the World Bank had released a report entitled, "Yemen – Towards a Water Strategy: An Agenda for Action," which recommended the following action points for addressing the impending water crisis:

---

[63] *Project Performance Assessment Report: Yemen.* World Bank, Feb. 2006, Report No. 35004.

[64] *Ibid.*

[65] Sahooly, Anwer. "Public-Private Partnership in the Water Supply and Sanitation Sector: The Experience of the Republic of Yemen." *International Journal of Water Resources Development* (Routledge, June 2003).

- Reforming macroeconomic policies in order to create the right signals for water conservation and efficiency;
- Generating consensus among political leaders;
- Harnessing private sector energies in urban water supply; and
- Approaching partnerships to engage rural water users in self-management of their own resources.[66]

The action steps proposed by the World Bank's report outline the framework for and establish the foundation of a PPP for urban water distribution. The report also recognized the need to address key components of successful PPPs including institutional capacity, political support, and viable incentives for private and public partners.

In 1999, the World Bank launched another project, the Sana'a Water Supply and Sanitation Project, whose aim was to implement the new substructure of the NWSA in Sana'a first, as outlined in the Cabinet Resolution 237, and set the pattern for other towns in Yemen to follow. The project was successful in achieving its goals of institutional reform; however, it made no attempt to address the more crucial problem of water resource depletion. [67]

The Cabinet Resolution established the following three-phased plan, to be implemented over ten years:

- *Phase I.* Restructuring the National Water and Sanitation Authority in order to decentralize the branches and allow them to set tariffs to fully cover costs, control income and expenditures, and recruit their own staff (with the exception of top management positions).
- *Phase II.* Transformation of some of the larger NWSA branches into local corporations operating according to

---

[66] Dervis, Kemal et. al. *Yemen - Toward a Water Strategy: An Agenda for Action* (World Bank, Aug. 1997), p. ii.
[67] *Project Performance Assessment Report: Yemen.* World Bank, Feb. 2006, Report No. 35004.

market principles through local, as opposed to central, management.

- *Phase III.* Incorporation of a PPP into the operation of each local corporation after identifying the most appropriate contractual arrangement through a dedicated study.[68]

The World Bank's Sana'a Water Supply and Sanitation Project implemented the three phases outlined by the Cabinet Resolution over four years, between 1999 and 2003. The Sana'a office of the NWSA was one of the first branches to become autonomous as a newly formed local corporation, known as the "Sana'a Water Supply and Sanitation Local Corporation" (hereinafter, "Sana'a Local Corporation"). With the legal transactions accompanying this development completed in 2001, the first task of the newly created Sana'a Local Corporation was to embark on capacity building measures in order to develop a skilled, dedicated workforce to oversee a future partnership, which was recommended by the World Bank in 1997 as a factor in the success of PPPs. This entailed the establishment of a financial department with computers and software to manage accounting; the development of technical training and detailed job descriptions for employees; the restructuring of compensation to include performance-based incentives; and the launching of tariff studies accompanied by plans to increase tariffs to cover operations and maintenance, thereby developing a dedicated revenue stream.[69]

By mid-2001, the Water and Sanitation Corporation was ready to begin the process of incorporating a PPP into its operations. The process was carried out with procedural oversight and substantive consultation from representatives of the International Development Association, particularly during the

---

[68] Sahooly, Anwer. "Public-Private Partnership in the Water Supply and Sanitation Sector: The Experience of the Republic of Yemen." *International Journal of Water Resources Development* (Routledge, June 2003).
[69] *Ibid.*

selection of the private sector partner and the development of the contract. The bidding schedule was set as follows:

- December 2001: the pre-qualification applications for prospective private contractors were released to applicants;
- January 2001: the applications were due.
- August 2002: requests for proposals were distributed to the pre-qualified applicants.
- March, 2003: the contract with the winning bidder would be awarded.[70]

Although the Sana'a Local Corporation followed the proposed schedule through January, 2003, it never entered into a formal PPP contract with a private firm for its operations.

After the success in incorporating an autonomous water supply and sanitation office in Sana'a, as well as professionally training the staff for operating the office, the World Bank determined that the Cabinet Resolution should be followed by other large cities in Yemen. The Urban Water Supply and Sanitation Project was launched in 2002, and its goal was to create local corporation for water supply and sanitation management in urban centers, including Ta'iz.[71] Another goal of the project was to include local participation in the establishment of the local water corporations.[72] This was mostly done through workshops in partnership with universities, donors, and the NWSA.

Along with the establishment of local water corporations, the Yemeni Parliament passed a new Water Law in 2002.[73] This law documented water rights for the first time, some following traditional negotiated water rights between villages and some

[70] *Ibid.*

[71] *Yemen - Project Appraisal Document for the First Phase of the Urban Water Supply & Sanitation Program.* World Bank, July, 2002, Report No. 24478-YEM.

[72] *Yemen: World Bank To Upgrade Water Supply, Sanitation Services.* World Bank, August 1, 2002, Press Release No. 2002/040/MENA.

[73] *A Partnership Approach to Sustainable Groundwater Management in Yemen.* Ministry of Water and Environment, Yemen. Fourth World Water Forum, Mexico, March, 2006.

establishing new limits to water usage. The government took further steps toward institution building in 2003 by creating a new Ministry of Water and Environment.[74]

In April of 2005, the government of Yemen and the World Bank each issued separate reports outlining a comprehensive strategy for the water sector. The National Water Sector Strategy and Investment Program (hereinafter, "NWSSIP") was issued by the Yemeni government and the Country Water Resource Assistance Strategy (hereinafter, "CWRAS") was issued by the World Bank.[75] These reports included such recommendations as enforcement of a licensing system for drilling contractors and enforcement of a well permits system. Both of these recommendations have been implemented successfully. For example, licensed drilling rigs are fixed with GPS technology to pinpoint there exact location at all times. Eventually, all rigs will be required to be stored at special drilling rig "parks," such that their movements can be controlled. Violations are published in the newspaper. All permitted wells are required to have a meter, and only group well permits are granted, in lieu of individual wells.

The reports also outline land and water conservation strategies. For example, the government subsidies for diesel fuel have been removed. This has effectively doubled the price of diesel, which is used to run groundwater pumps. This has encouraged more group well permit applications, and has also encouraged farmers to plant crops that use less water, as the value of the crop cultivation is now tied to each drop of water required to grow it.[76]

After almost a decade of restructuring the water sector's institutional framework, the first PPP in Yemen was signed in 2006

---

[74] *Ibid.*

[75] *Project Performance Assessment Report: Yemen.* World Bank, Feb. 2006, Report No. 35004.

[76] *A Partnership Approach to Sustainable Groundwater Management in Yemen.* Ministry of Water and Environment, Yemen. Fourth World Water Forum, Mexico, March, 2006.

between the Netherlands Ministry for Development Cooperation, the Ta'iz Water Supply and Sanitation Local Corporation, and Vitens N.V., the largest drinking water supply company in the Netherlands.[77] The agreement is not as that which was proposed for Sana'a four years earlier, in 2002, which was for a private corporation to operate the local water corporation. Rather, the agreement in Ta'iz is what is known as a *performance based professional support* partnership.[78] However, whereas in a typical performance based partnership, the supportee would pay the fee of the supporter, the fee for Vitens services in Ta'iz are being paid by several members of the international donor community in Yemen, including the Netherlands Ministry for Development Cooperation. The "performance-based" partnership implies that Vitens will take a loss in the early stages of the contract, but will recuperate its losses as the Ta'iz Water Supply and Sanitation Local Corporation reaches certain benchmarks. The benchmarks being applied to the local water corporations in Yemen have been established through the work of GTZ, the German Development Corporation.

---

[77] "Development Cooperation." Embassy of the Kingdom of the Netherlands in Sana'a, Republic of Yemen, November 16, 2008, available at http://yemen.nlembassy.org/development.

[78] Van Ginneken, Meike. *Improving Performance through Bilateral Utility Partnerships*. World Bank Water Operators Partnership Workshop, Johannesburg, April 2007.

Actions by the International Donor Community:

Actions by the Government of Yemen:

1992 - Land and Water rural irrigation technology program
World Bank

1995 - Multi Donor Group for Yemen Water formed
UNDP, World Bank, and the Netherlands
World Water Conservation Project

1996 - Ta'iz Water Supply pipes groundwater into Ta'iz from rural farms
World Bank

1995 - 1997 - Preparation with Ministry of Electricity and Water
GTZ consults with Ministry of Electricity and Water Pilot Project

1997 - Yemen - Towards a Water Strategy: An Agenda for Action
World Bank report outlining PPPs in local water sector
structural recommendations

1999 - Sana'a Water Supply and Sanitation Project
World Bank to implement CR 237 in Sana'a

2002 - Urban Water Supply and Sanitation Project
World Bank to implement CR 237 throughout Yemen

2005 - Country Water Resource Assistance Strategy
World Bank report for comprehensive water sector strategies

1995 - National Water and Sanitation Authority
Government of Yemen creates new central
planning agency for water management

1997 - Cabinet Resolution 237
Government of Yemen mandates new structure for NWSA

2002 - Water Law
Government of Yemen creates new regulation over water rights

2003 - Ministry of Water and Environment
Government of Yemen creates new cabinet office

2005 - National Water Sector Strategy and Investment Program
Government of Yemen report for comprehensive
water sector strategies

2006 - Public Private Partnership
Signed in Ta'iz
The Netherlands, Vitens N.V.,
and Ta'iz local water corporation
sign a performance based
professional support partnership

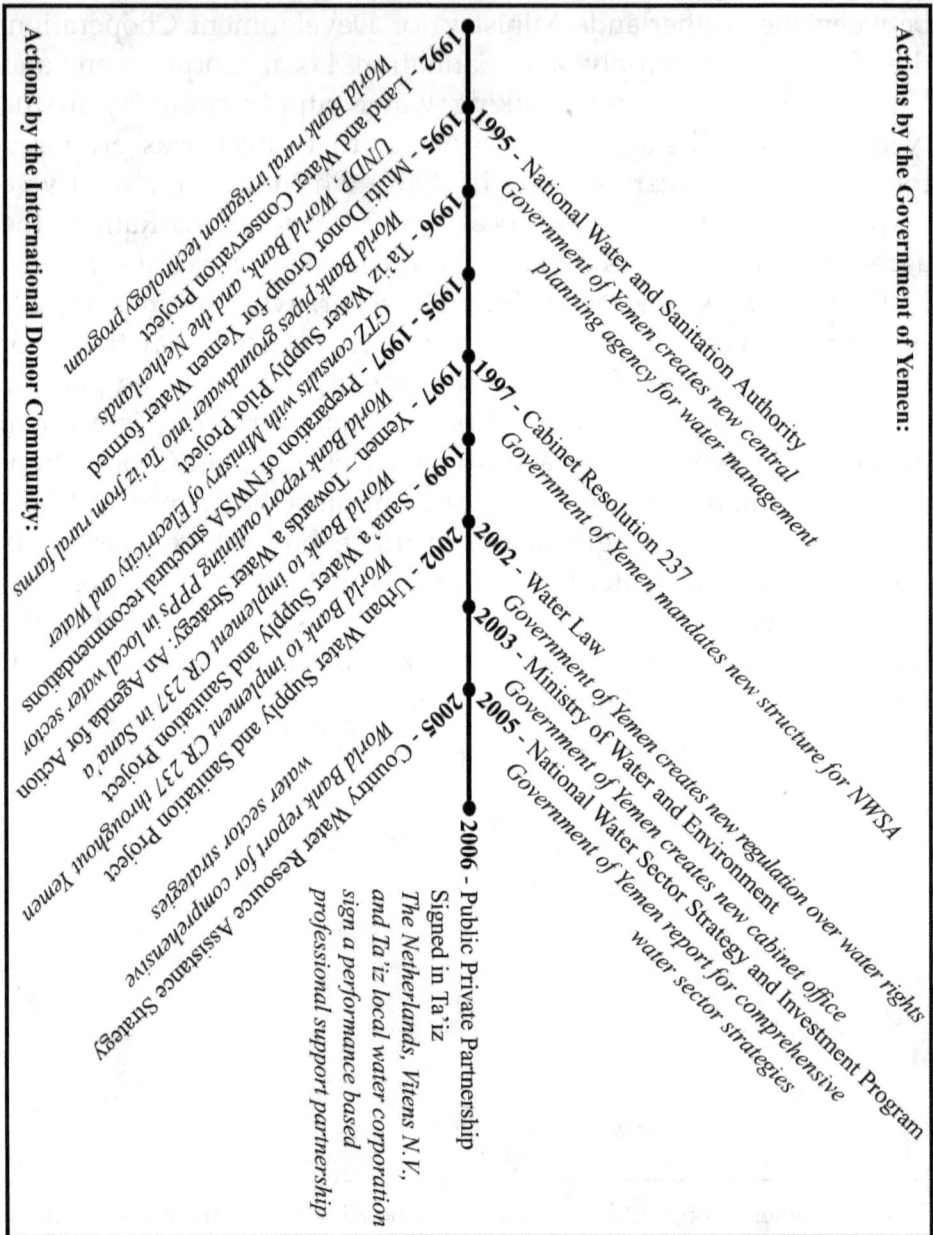

Clearly, the international donor community has had its hand
in every aspect of the Yemeni water sector reforms of the last

decade. Great consideration for coordinating efforts has brought a total change to the institutional framework regulating water resources consumption. Although it is perhaps too early to determine whether these reforms will be successful in raising the human development level in Yemen, there is hope that with better water resource management Yemen's future will not be dashed by drought, famine and massive resettlement.

5.2 Principles for Successful Development

The depletion of water resources is a major obstacle to Yemen's future development, since it will lead to population resettlement, rural to urban migration, and crop failure. Even the absence of piped water for over fifty percent of the population is a drain on development resources, as the burden of time and energy required to fetch water is often born by women. Women in Yemen are over seventy percent illiterate because they are often overburdened with time intensive housework even as children and are not sent to school. The lack of educational choice and achievement by women in Yemen has greatly lowered Yemen's Human Development score. Any improvement in water delivery and water resources conservation directly impacts the status of women as contributors in an increasingly literacy-dependent society. In this way, the water sector reforms of the World Bank in Yemen "fit" a problem that has impeded advancement.

The lion's share of the international donor community's work in Yemen's water sector has been in building the institutions necessary to sustain reforms in water consumption and water delivery services. This work has been successful, though it has been performed over ten years. The slow implementation of institutional restructuring has contributed to a *stable* transition from an uncoordinated and inefficient central water agency to multiple autonomous local water corporations and one national regulatory agency (the NWSA).

While these multiple projects have been successful at building new institutions, they have not been built under the initiative of the Yemeni people. In fact, most of the steps taken by the government of Yemen toward water sector reform were at the direct recommendation of the international donor community. Not to diminish the role of consultants in development work, but there is little evidence that these programs have encouraged the Yemeni people to mobilize themselves in tackling challenges to their own development. Even the World Bank rhetoric on public participation for successful development only amounted to a series of workshops sponsored by the international community. This raises serious concern over Yemen's ability to face the challenges that are inevitable in the future without continuous coaching from their international donors.

Similarly, the requirements placed on Yemen's government to receive international aid do not appear to exceed minimum cooperation with the donor's agenda. While the private corporation providing professional services to the Ta'iz local water corporation will be compensated according to their performance, it does not appear that there are similar benchmarks for Yemen's government to meet in order to secure international loans from the World Bank, other than to cooperate with their programs. Without competition for funds, there is little incentive to perform.

5.3   Public Private Partnership

Although the World Bank had been trying to establish a PPP in Yemen's water sector since 1997, it is a stretch to qualify the agreement signed in 2006 between the Netherlands, the Ta'iz local water corporation, and Vitens N.V. as a PPP. Under the World Bank's financial structure, when a project is approved for a certain dollar amount, funds are transferred to the recipient government with stipulations as to how the monies should be spent. A significant portion is usually designated for consultant fees. The recipient government is encouraged to put out requests for proposals for consultant work from qualified agencies around the globe. The awarded consultant contract is then paid for with money from the World Bank project loan.

In the case of the Ta'iz PPP, the structure is very similar to the usual pattern of procuring World Bank consultant contracts. The private firm, Vitens N.V., is providing professional services. The Ta'iz local water corporation is the recipient of those services, and the fees are being paid by the international donor community. Why this agreement should be considered a PPP when the World Bank-funded consultant contracts are not remains a question in this author's mind. The only difference is that the fees are tied to the performance of the Ta'iz local water corporation that results from the professional services of Vitens, N.V.

The agreement was brokered by the Netherlands Ministry for Development Cooperation. The total project cost is €1.65 million; the project duration is from 2006 to 2009. The Netherlands provided €950,000 in grants towards the project; the Yemeni government provided €200,000 toward the project, and the Vitens, N.V. has donated €500,000 in man hours toward the project. The project negotiations did not include participation from the general public. The partnership implementation process did not contribute to increasing Yemen's human development potential.

Chapter 6.

UNITED ARAB EMIRATES: THE NGO LAW AND

CIVIC ENGAGEMENT

6.1   General Overview

6.1.1   Introduction

The legal regime governing nongovernmental organizations (NGOs) in the United Arab Emirates is in many ways more restrictive than those governing NGOs in the US and other western jurisdictions. Although the state provides financial support to properly registered NGOs, the extent of activities that may be undertaken by local NGOs is limited by regulations that require the NGOs to apply for permissions to undertake new projects and activities and that prohibit NGOs from receiving funds from sources from outside of the UAE.

In the UAE, NGOs are usually referred to as "associations" or "societies for public welfare." Although there are only about one hundred NGOs in the nation, the sector includes a number of well-funded philanthropic organizations that work internationally.

Registration with the Ministry of Labor and Social Affairs is required for all NGOs operating in the UAE. After registration, some NGOs may receive subsidies from the government based on the membership size. Approximately 100 domestic NGOs were registered with the Ministry in 2008. However, despite this requirement, more than 20 unregistered local NGOs focused on non-political topics operate with little or no government interference.[79]

---

[79] See http://www.state.gov/g/drl/rls/hrrpt/2005/61701.htm.

The percentage of citizen membership in NGOs varies widely. All private associations and charitable groups require approval and licensing by local authorities, although this requirement is enforced loosely in some Emirates.[80]

6.1.2 Legal Framework

Federal Law No. (2) of 2008 in respect of National Societies and Associations of Public Welfare, which replaces Federal Law No. (6) of 1974 and its amending laws, defines and provides the framework for public welfare organizations operating within the UAE. Youth organizations fall under Law No. 25 of 1999.[81]

The primary regulator of public welfare organizations operating across the UAE is the Ministry of Labour and Social Affairs. The Department of Islamic Affairs and Charitable Activities provides licenses to those organizations operating in Dubai only. Before issuing a license, the Department seeks approval from the Ministry of Labour and Social Affairs.[82]

In addition, the "International Humanitarian City" (IHC) in Dubai counts a number of international NGOs among its members. The IHC was set up by Royal Decree – Law No. 6 of 2007 Establishing the International Humanitarian City, which formed the city as a free zone. Details of the membership requirements are available on the IHC website.

Organizations hosted by the IHC are not required to register with the Ministry of Labour and Social Affairs or the Department of Islamic Affairs and Charitable Activities Department, unless they plan to fundraise or carry out work within the UAE. Many

---

[80] *Ibid.*

[81] See http://www.ngoregnet.org/country_information_by_region/Middle_East_and_North_Africa/United_Arab_ Emirates.asp.

[82] See the licensing rules published at http://www.iacad.gov.ae/admin/storage/other/htmlDocs/Rules%20of%20Religious.doc for details.

organizations looking to work in the Gulf have thus registered in the IHC. However, by doing so, their ability to work freely in the UAE is restricted.

Currently approximately 37 NGOs are listed as members in the IHC. Among these, three are Emirati organizations.

6.1.3 NGO Sector

An estimated 120 public welfare societies are registered in the UAE and supervised by the Ministry of Labour and Social Affairs. The majority of these societies focus on social and humanitarian issues; others focus on professional and religious matters. The Ministry has recently launched an internet site called Musahama, which lists all NGOs and charities in the UAE. In the Emirate of Dubai the Department of Islamic Affairs and Charitable Activities lists 13 organizations on its publicly available register.

6.2 Reporting Requirements

Public welfare societies or associations are required to submit annual financial accounts to the Ministry of Labour and Social Affairs 15 days after they have been approved by the organization's Annual General Assembly. The Department of Islamic Affairs and Charitable Activities requires organizations it registers to provide annual reports of its activities along with financial accounts. The department audits each society's accounts.

The IHC also requires its members to provide reports of their activities and financial reports when they apply for their annual license.

6.3 Freedom of NGOs in the UAE

The government has established certain censorship regulations that curb the liberty of associations to publish freely. Such associations must follow the government's censorship guidelines and receive prior government approval before publishing materials. Participation by NGO members in any event outside the country is subsidized. *Participants must however obtain government permission before attending such events, even if they are not speakers.* The extent to which the government denies permissions to applicants is unknown, but it is likely that applications to attend events dealing with sensitive political, religious, or economic themes would be routinely denied.

Although the legal regimes impose a great deal of restrictions on the work and projects that NGOs may undertake, in practice, these restrictions, if violated, are often overlooked.[83]

6.4 Nongovernmental Investigations of Alleged Violations of Human Rights

The only local human rights organization in the UAE is the government-subsidized and government-affiliated Jurists' Association Human Rights Committee, which focuses on human rights education and conducts seminars and symposia, subject to government approval.

In July 2004, a group of citizens petitioned the Ministry of Labor and Social Affairs to approve the registration of an independent human rights NGO, the UAE Human Rights Society. Although the Ministry, by its own regulation, is required to act on all such applications within 30 days of receipt, it had not acted by the end of the year. The Ministry also had not acted on an application filed in April by a second group, the Emirates Association for Human Rights, seeking human rights NGO status.[84]

The failure to act on these applications is seen by some as a further manifestation of the government's desire to exercise close control over associations dealing with potentially controversial topics.

---

[83] See http://www.state.gov/g/drl/rls/hrrpt/2005/61701.htm.
[84] See http://www.state.gov/g/drl/rls/hrrpt/2005/61701.htm.

PART 3.
CONCLUSIONS AND RECOMMENDATIONS

Public private partnerships remain a flexible means of both economically and socially advancing societies. However, in the field of international development, PPPs are still entrenched in privatization ideology, as can be observed in the case in Yemen. PPPs, as can be observed in case studies, have the potential to be successful regardless of whether they are initiated by a public partner or private partner. As long as the partnership is directly linked to the challenges and issues hindering a community's advancement, the strength of both the private and public sectors can be joined in meeting those challenges.

PPPs also contribute to building human organization, since groups of people must first organize before they can enter into contracts, as clearly shown in the Dudley case. The Emilia Romagna case further offers an example that built human organization, since the industrial sector service centers provided the venue for diverse partnerships to be formed between small businesses, financial institutions, the government, and between small businesses in the same sector. This eventually led to the development of flexible manufacturing, a unique network among small businesses whereby they collaborate to submit joint bids for large contracts. The flexible structure of PPPs endues them with the potential to engage civil society in development planning and ownership.

The success of PPPs in international development depends upon whether they incorporate the fundamental principles of successful development, such as human organization, managed competition to reduce corruption, institution building, the design of solutions to fit the problem, and social, political and economic stability. These are the same principles that international development programs of all types are dependent on.

Chapter 7.

RECOMMENDATIONS FOR DEVELOPMENT PRACTICE

The principles identified in the literature review and tested in the case studies are significant to successful development strategies. As demonstrated in the World Bank's involvement in Yemen's water sector, maintaining stability when implementing changes is of great importance. For this reason, small incremental changes, which minimize the risk of incurring great social costs in project implementation, were made in restructuring the country's water resource management system.

Human organization is the engine the drives development. When people begin to coordinate their activities, they reach higher levels of efficiency and production. These connections among people are also the means of sustaining social and economic advancements, as they eventually evolve into the institutions that are appropriately designed to maintain newfound development levels.

Minimizing corruption and promoting transparent processes are indispensable to equitable development. Managed competition creates an environment where competitors are each treated equally, and no competitor is given an unfair advantage over others. An improvement on this basic arrangement is one where competitors are also encouraged to collaborate while retaining their individual identities (collaboration of competitors should not be confused with a merger). This more sophisticated system of managed competition reinforces checks and balances among competitors, minimizing corruption and promoting transparency.

Conclusions and Recommendations

Finally, including the people most impacted by a development scheme as participants in planning the development project directly impacts the success of the project. Any development project that claims to be for the betterment of a society but, when implemented, benefits less individuals than it harms, has missed its mission. Participation in development planning by the recipients of the development strategies helps the design of solutions meet the challenges that have impeded their advancement. Successful development occurs when solutions are designed to fit specific problems and are effective in eliminating those problems.

Chapter 8.

RECOMMENDATIONS FOR FURTHER STUDY

Overall, the international development community, namely, the World Bank, the IMF, and other international donors, have been deficient in implementing public participation in development planning and in creating a structure for managed competition among donees. A better understanding of the World Bank-sponsored community workshops — the primary means of engaging citizens in development planning participation in some nations, and how they are conducted might reveal more about the true measure of public participation in the planning process. If these workshops could be structured to reflect the pattern set in the Dudley case, where the community participated in the development of the Neighborhood Comprehensive Revitalization Plan, they could maximize the future success of the project implementation, as those engaged in project planning are the same individuals most affected by the project's implementation.

Further study into how the principles of managed competition can be introduced into the existing financial structures of the World Bank would be worth pursuing. Excluding the small grant program that the World Bank has recently initiated, the loans that the Bank makes to national governments do not involve competition for development funds. Once funds are transferred to a national government, the means of assuring that the funds reach their targeted recipients and do not end up in the pockets of public officials is dependent only on World Bank oversight and not on a system of checks and balances. Corruption has been a major roadblock to development in many less developed countries. Introducing managed competition into the mechanisms of international aid would greatly improve the success of international development projects.

EXCERPTS OF THE NGO LAWS OF THE UNITED ARAB EMIRATES

Federal Law No. (2) of 2008 in Respect of the National Societies and Associations of Public Welfare

We, Khalifa Bin Zayed Al Nahyan, the President of the United Arab Emirates,
- Upon reviewing the constitution,
- The Federal Law No. (1) of 1972 regarding the ministries' jurisdictions, ministers' authorities, and the laws amending thereof,
- The Federal Law No. (12) of 1972 regulating the societies and associations operating in the field of youth care,
- The Federal Law No. (6) of 1974 in respect of the public welfare societies, and the laws amending thereof,
- The Federal Law No. (25) of 1999 related to the Youth Welfare and Sports General Authority,
- And based on the presentations submitted by the minister of Social Affairs, and the approvals of the Council of Ministers, as well as the Federal National Council, and on the sanction of the Supreme Council of the Federation ,
We do hereby enact the following law:

Preamble Chapter
Definitions
Article (1)
For the purpose of implementing the provisions of this law, the following phrases and words shall have the meanings assigned

opposite each of them as shown hereunder unless otherwise is
required by the context .

The State	The United Arab Emirates
The Ministry	The Ministry of Social Affairs
The Minister	The Minister of Social Affairs
The Society	The Society of Public Welfare
The Union	An assembly having more than one Society of Public Welfare
The Board	The Union or Society's Board of Directors
The Member	The Society's Member
The National Foundation	Any foundation having one founder or a group of founders, established for a limited or an unlimited period by allocating certain funds for the achievement of one of the purposes stipulated under Article (2) herein, without seeking financial profits.

Article (2)
In implementation of the provisions of this law, the society of
public welfare means any assembly (group) having a regulation
valid for a limited or unlimited period, comprising natural or
artificial persons, for the purpose of achieving a social, religious,
cultural, scientific, educational, professional, feminine, innovative,
or an artistic activity, or provision of humanitarian services, or for
serving a charity or consolidation purpose, whether through
financial or moral assistance, or by know-how, seeking in all its

activities achievement of Public Welfare without obtaining financial profit, and having its membership open for everybody under the provisions of this law. The importance of specifying the objective of the society is represented by the chief purpose for which it has been established.

Chapter One
Incorporation of the Society [Association]

Article (3)
To incorporate the society, the following requirements shall be met:
1. Number of the founders shall not be less than twenty members. However, the Minister may apply exceptions in this condition, permitting the number of such founders to be not less than five members.
2. The age of the member should not be less than Eighteen Years.
3. The member should enjoy good conduct and reputation and never been convicted of imprisonment due to committing a felony or a misuse of trust or honor misdemeanor unless he / she is already rehabililitated.
4. All the founder members and staff shall be holders of the United Arab Emirates citizenship. The aforesaid conditions shall be applied to the societies comprising artificial persons to the extent such conditions can be applied thereto.

Article (4)
The founders shall hold an assembly for setting out the society's Articles of Association including the following details:
1. The name of the society derived from its objective, place of its headquarters and scope of activity in the State, provided that such a name does not arouse confusion with another society operating within the scope of its activity.
2. Objectives of the Society.

3. Membership conditions and categories, with the procedures of its acceptance and forfeiture, as well as the rights and duties of members.
4. The manner of forming the board of directors, its functions and the work system therein.
5. Rules and principles for regulating the ordinary or extraordinary general assemblies, their functions, assembly invitation procedures and the conditions for valid convention.
6. Rules for amending the society's articles of association, establishing branches or centers affiliated thereto, or merging the same with other societies, in addition to rules of membership and participation in the bodies, organizations, and conferences outside the State.
7. Resources of the society and the manner of utilizing the same, disposing of them and the method of controlling of spending thereof, beginning and end of its fiscal year, the system for retaining advances and the values thereof for meeting the urgent expenditures, as well as the rules for raising donations.
8. The conditions for winding the society up voluntarily, rules of its liquidation and the decision regarding its funds.
The Ministry shall prepare a model society Articles of Association to be used for guidance.

...

Chapter Four
The Private Fund

Article 44
The founders shall set out articles of association of the Private Fund, including the following information:
1. Name of the Fund with its geographical scope of operation, and its headquarters inside the State.
2. The objective for which the Fund is incorporated
3. A detailed statement on the funds allocated for realizing the objectives of the Fund.

4. Organization of the Fund's management including the manner of appointing the chairman and the members of the Board of Trustees as well as appointing the director.

The Private Fund may be incorporated under an official instrument (document) or under an authenticated will, where both shall be deemed as articles of association for such a Fund. A model statute of the Private Funds shall be enclosed with the executive bylaw of this Law to be used as a reference.

Article 45

The Private Fund shall be managed by a board of trustees according to its articles of association, and shall be represented by the Chairman of the board of trustees before the courts and third party.

Article 46

The Private Funds shall be subject to the provisions stipulated under this law and its executive bylaw, as may be appropriate to their nature, for any matters not stipulated for under this chapter.

...

Rules for Licenses of Religious and Charitable Societies and Organization of their Activities in the Emirate of Dubai, Islamic Affairs & Chartable Activities Department of the Government of Dubai

IN THE NAME OF ALLAH, THE MOST GRACIOUS, MOST MERCIFUL

Resolution Number (12) for the year 2006
Rules for Licenses of Religious and
Charitable Societies and Organization
Of their Activities in the Emirate of Dubai

Chapter one

After reviewing Law # (12) for the year 2005 regarding the formation of the Department of Islamic Affairs & Charitable Activities Department.

And Decree # (20) for the year 2002 regarding the appointment of a general manager for Islamic Affairs & Charitable Activities Department in Dubai.

And after reviewing Federal Law # (6) for the year 1974 for the public benefit societies and its amendments.

It is decided to issue the following rules:

Article (1):
These rules are called (Rules for Licenses of Religious and Charitable Societies and Organization of their Activities in the Emirate of Dubai) and their provisions shall be applicable on all the religious and charitable societies.

Definitions

Article (2):

In application of the provisions of these rules the following shall mean:

The Country	:	United Arab Emirates.
The Emirate	:	Emirate of Dubai.
The Ministry	:	Ministry of Labor and Social Affairs The
Department	:	Islamic Affairs & Chartable

Activities Department

The manager	:	General Manager of the Department
The rules	:	Rules for Licenses of

Religious and Charitable Societies and Organization of their Activities in the Emirate of Dubai.

The society : Every organization or establishment or a   society dealing in religious or charitable activities as per the definitions stipulated by these rules, and which performs its activities permanently or temporarily in the Emirate of Dubai under Law # (12) for the year 2005 regarding the formation of Islamic Affairs & Chartable Activities Department

Section one

Rules for Licenses of Religious and Charitable Societies

Firstly: Classification of Societies:
Article (3):

They are classified as follows:

Excerpts of the NGO Laws of the United Arab Emirates

1-   The religious society: it is the society formed for the purpose of the call for Islamic religion and spreading it among non-Muslims or to guide Muslims to its teachings, and make them aware about their religion and to take care of Islamic culture. The society in order to achieve this shall exercise the following activities for example:

      a-   Distribution of the Holy Quran.

      b-   To issue books,   magazines   and   periodicals specialized in the call for Islam and Sharia science in   the different languages, and distribution of the same,   and   to produce and distribute reading, audio or   video materials on the suitable media.

      c-   To convene exhibitions, conferences,   and presentations, to organize studies, Sharia,   educational and religious lectures.

      d-   Preparation   of   researches,   Sharia   and jurisprudence studies.

2-   The charitable society: It is the society formed for the purposes of collecting donations (alms) in cash or in kind, and spending of the same in the charitable activities inside or outside the State.   These societies perform the following activities for example:

      a-   Building of Mosques, schools, hospitals, clinics and care centers.

      b-   To build roads and to dig wells etc.

      c-   Collection of donations (alms) and Zakat and to distribute the same to those who are entitled.

      d-   To take care of Doat (callers for the spread of Islam), and to provide financial assistance to needy students.

      e-   To take care of and sponsor orphans, elders and special need individuals.

f-   Preparation of pilgrims and those intending to perform Omra.

g-   Slaughter of religious sacrifice (Adhahi) and distribution of their meats.

h-   Convening of charitable exhibitions.

The society may practice both religious and charitable activity, as per what is stated in paragraphs (1) and (2) above, provided that it possesses the prerequisites to practice activities in both fields, and that it obtains a license for that from the Department.

Article (4):

 The society may not practice any activity contrary to the provisions of these rules, and the objectives stated in the society's articles of association. The society shall not perform the following works and activities in particular:

1-   Performance of political activities or adoption of certain political attitudes or to support political movements.

2-   To instigate sectarian, racial or partisan or intellectual or ideological differences.

3-   To perform any commercial business by itself, except the investment of the endowments put under its disposal.

4-   To attempt to obtain profits in exchange for performing its activities.

5-   To use the funds in purposes for which they are not intended.

Article (5):

The society whatever its type shall do the following:

1-   Develop its work through the invention of new practices and the use of new technologies and methods in management and regulation.

2-   Co-operation and co-ordination with other similar parties inside the State to develop its activities.

3-   The society can co-operate with related and recognized regional and international parties in order to perform its objectives, and in order to assist it in completing its work programs outside the State, provided that the department shall be provided with a list of the parties with whom dealings are made, for obtaining prior approval of the same.

Article (6):
The society shall provide the financial, administrative and technical requirements necessary to perform its activities and in particular it shall provide the following requirements:

1-   The society shall have an equipped location to perform the administrative, financial and organizational activities in the Emirate of Dubai, provided the following conditions are complied with:

   a-   A suitable location to carry out the general activities.
   b-   The location shall be equipped with furniture, office and technical equipments necessary for performing the religious or charitable activities.

2-   The society shall have a qualified manager who shall be responsible for its management. It shall also have its financial system and an accountant who shall be responsible for the accounts and the financial procedures, and he shall possess the professional and scientific qualifications and the necessary practical experience to perform his duties.

3-   The society shall have a staff of full time or part time employees or of volunteers who possess the professional and scientific qualifications and the necessary practical experience to perform management or financial or religious activities.

4-   All this shall be made through co-ordination with the concerned parties.

Secondly: Licenses of Societies
1-   Licenses of the society of public benefit:

Article (7):
The founder of the society established in the Emirate of Dubai as a society of public benefit, shall submit the formation application to the Department which the following documents shall be attached:

1-   The name, address and location of the society.

2-   A study showing all the aspects related to the system and work method of the society.

3-   Statement about the names of founders, their capacity, addresses and copies of their passports.

4-   A copy of the proposed articles of association of the society.

Article (8):
1-   The concerned department shall study the application for formation of the society according to the following:
        a- Availability of the prerequisites in the founding members, and the members of the proposed board of

directors in terms of legal capacity and ability to carry out voluntary work.

b- Scope of work and activities which shall be performed by the society, which are stated in its articles of association.

c- The society shall work according to the regulations setup by the Department for the organization of religious and charitable activities.

d- Completion of all official documents.

2-   The Department is entitled to request meeting with the founding members to check all aspects, which it sees necessary to be checked.

3-   The Department shall send a letter to the Ministry of Labor and Social Affairs either for preliminary approval for the formation of the society or for the rejection of the same.

4-   The Department is entitled to consider the formation application and to issue its resolution either for acceptance of rejection within a period not exceeding two months from the date of receiving the formation application.

Article (9):

The preliminary approval of the Department shall not be considered as a license to perform the activities, and the society shall not perform any activities until completion of its formation procedures, and its announcement by the Ministry of Labor and Social Affairs, as per the provisions of Federal law # (6) for the year 1974, regarding the societies of public benefit and its amendments, then completion of its licensing procedures by the Department, according to the provisions stipulated by these rules, or any laws or legislations applicable at the time of the announcement.

Article (10):

1-   The society after completion of the procedures of   its formation and announcement by the Ministry of Labor and Social Affairs,   shall provide the Department with the announcement resolution and   the articles of association to be approved by the Department, or to make the appropriate amendments on the same as per these rules, and the address of the location of the society in which the activities are performed, in order to complete licensing procedures by the Department,   and   the society shall not be entitled to perform its activities   before obtaining final approval from the Department.

2- The Department shall issue the license after making sure that all conditions are fulfilled.

3- The society shall renew its license at the Department once every two years for charitable societies. As for religious societies, license shall be renewed each year before the expiry date.

4- If the society applies any clause of article 4 of these rules, coordination shall be made with the Ministry to apply the appropriate action against it.

2-   Licenses for the society formed in the Emirate by a party or an individual:

Article (11):

The society formed in the Emirate by an individual or an official or private party, shall be directly licensed by the Department as per the terms and conditions and the procedures stated in these rules.

Article (12):

The society, which is formed as an individual establishment shall possess the following prerequisites:

Excerpts of the NGO Laws of the United Arab Emirates

1-   The founder shall be an Emirates national, and shall have the legal capacity. If the founder is an artificial person, it shall be licensed according to the provisions of the law governing the activities of that party.

2-   The founder shall possess the financial ability to fund the activities of the society.

3-   The society shall have one or more banking accounts if necessary, and its accounts shall be separate from those of the founder.

4-   The society shall not collect donations for financing its activities even if they are charitable activities, unless it obtains a written approval from the Department.

5-   The society shall pay its charitable assistance inside the State according to regular records showing the names of beneficiaries. If assistance is paid outside the State, the payment shall be made by another charitable society approved by the Department.

Article (13):
The founder of the society, which is formed by an individual or a party, or his representative, shall submit to the Department the application for formation and licensing of the society, and the following documents shall be attached to the application

1-   The name, address and location of the society.

2-   The proposed articles of association of the society stating the objectives of the society.

3-   A study showing all the aspects related to the to the formation of the society and its work methods.

4-   The organizational structure of the society, and the distribution of assignments and responsibilities.

5-   A list of the names of members of the proposed board of directors, and copies of their passports, provided that all the members of the board shall be form the citizens of the United Arab Emirates.

Article (14):
The Department shall study the license application for the society as per the provisions and procedures stated in article 8 of these rules, and the license shall be issued according to that. The society shall renew its license at the Department once every two years for charitable societies. As for religious societies, license shall be renewed each year before the expiry date

1- The proposed articles of association of the society, signed by the founding members.

2- The organizational structure of the society, and the distribution of assignments and responsibilities.

3- A study showing all the aspects related to the organization and work method of the society.

4- Copies of passports of the founding members with valid a residence issued by Dubai.

5- Minutes of meetings of the general assembly.

6- Resolution of the general assembly authorizing its representative at the Department to follow up the licensing procedures.

7- Certificate of good conduct.

Provisions for the Formation and Licensing of Religious Societies of Foreign Communities:

Article (15):

Religious societies formed in the Emirate of Dubai by individuals representing one of the Islamic communities residing in the Emirate, by the Department as per the formation and licensing procedures stipulated by these rules, and shall possess the following prerequisites:

1- The founders shall not be less than twenty members, but if necessary, they can be less than that according to the approval of the Department.

2- This community shall not have another society licensed in the Emirate of Dubai at the time of the application.

3- The founders shall adhere to all the provisions included in these rules.

Article (16) :

The founders of the society shall nominate from among them the person who shall represent them in following up the licensing procedures stipulated by these rules, and they shall submit to the Department a written application for the formation of the society with which the following documents shall be attached:

1- The proposed articles of association of the society signed by the founding members.

2- The society's organizational structure and the distribution of specializations and responsibilities.

3- A study showing all the aspects related to the organization of the society and its method of work.

4- Passport copies of the founding members with a valid residence visa issued in Dubai.

5- Minutes of meeting of the constituent assembly.

6- Resolution of the constituent assembly of authorizing its representative to follow up the licensing procedures.

7- A certificate of good conduct.

Article (17):
The Department shall study the application for licensing the society submitted by the founders, after finalization of all the required official documents.

Article (18):
1- The Department shall send a letter to the founders stating whether or not the preliminary approval is given.
2- In case of approval, the society shall not conduct its business unless all licensing procedures are finalized by the Department.

3- The society shall renew its license at the Department before one month at least from the expiry date.

Excerpts of the NGO Laws of the United Arab Emirates

4-   The formation and management of the society shall be governed by the provisions of these rules.

Section two
Licenses of branches of Societies

Article (19):
The branches of the society formed and operating in the Emirate of Dubai shall be licensed inside the Emirate directly by the Department, and the following provisions and procedures stipulated later in these rules shall be applicable to them.

Article (20):
The society licensed in the State shall submit an application to the Department for opening its branch inside the Emirate, and the following conditions shall be applied:

1-   The society shall be operating at the time of the application.

2-   The society shall be financially capable of bearing the expenses of opening and management of the branch.

3-   The board of directors of the society shall have justified reasons to open the branch.

Article (21):
1-   The Department shall study the application, in terms of the availability of the above conditions,   verifying the performance level of the society.

2-   The Department shall send a letter to the society of approval or rejection within a period not exceeding two months from the date of application.

3-   After completion of the documents procedures of the branch license, the Department shall issue the license. The society shall renew the license at the Department once a year before its expiry date.

Dissolution of the society

Article (22):

Apart from the society formed as a society for public benefit the society can be optionally dissolved by a resolution of the extra – ordinary general assembly, or by the concerned party in the Department, provided that the Department shall be notified in writing about the place and date of the general assembly before fifteen days, and the Department shall coordinate with the ministry in this connection.

Article (23):

1-   The Department can dissolve the society through coordination with the ministry in the following cases:

a-   If it is discovered that its activities contradict or do   not   achieve its objectives, or if the society becomes   incapable of achieving its objectives.

b-   If it disposes of its funds in purposes, contrary to those   which are originally stipulated.

c-   If it becomes unable to fulfill its financial obligations.

d-   If it does not keep its records and documents according to article 47 of these rules, or if such records willfully contain incorrect statements.

e-   If the society commits a serious violation of the provisions of these rules or of its articles of association.

2-   The Department is entitled to take the necessary procedures to refer the violations, which require judicial judgments to the concerned authority to take the necessary legal procedures with respect to the violations referred to in the previous paragraph.

Chapter two

Section one

Financial resources of societies and method of   spending

1-   Financial resources of religious societies:

Article (24):

The financial resources of religious societies, on which they depend to finance their activities, consist of the following:

1-   Subscriptions of the members.

2-   Personal grants given by the founder of the society, in the case of the society formed by a certain individual or party.

3-   Financial grants given to the society, which are accepted by the society's board of directors, and which shall not contradict the society's objectives and legal purposes.

4-   Testaments and endowments which are left under the disposal of the society.

5-   The proceeds of the presentations and parties and other activities carried out by the society, provided that the income of these events is dedicated to finance the society's activities.

6-   Any other revenues, which do not contradict the nature of the activity of the religious society, and which is approved by the Department.

7-   All the above is subject to the prior approval of the
      Department, before starting any activity.

Financial resources of charitable societies and how to collect the
same:

Article (25):

The financial resources of charitable societies, on which they
depend to finance their activities, consist of the following:

1- Subscriptions of the members.

2- Personal grants given by the founder of the society, in the
   case of the society formed by a certain individual or party.

3- The proceeds of the presentations and parties and
   campaigns and other activities carried out by the society.

4- Cash and in kind donations collected by the society as per
   the provisions of these rules.

5- Grants given to the society as per the provisions of these
   rules.

6- Testaments and endowments which are left under the
   disposal of the society.

7- Alms and Zakat.

8- Any other revenues, which do not contradict the nature of
   the activity of the society, or its objectives, and which are
   approved by the board of directors.

Article (26):

Excerpts of the NGO Laws of the United Arab Emirates

The charitable societies may collect donations and cash and in kind alms, using one or more of the following practices, provided that the provisions included in these rules shall be adhered to:

1- Performance of the parties and campaigns for the charitable activities, and collection of donations from the participants.

2- To advertise through the different advertisement media.

3- Collection of donations through sponsorship.

4- Other legal methods, which do not contradict the laws of the state, provided the prior approval of the Department is obtained before starting the work.

Donations collection procedures by boxes

Article (27):
The charitable societies shall adhere to the following conditions upon collection of donations and in cash alms:

1- The society shall obtain a written approval from the party in which location donations shall be collected as follows:

   a- Mosques: Islamic Affairs & Charitable Activities Department.
   b- Public utilities such as the open markets and parks: Dubai Municipality
   c- Commercial outlets and centres: management of the centre or the outlet or the commercial complex.
   d- Governmental and private establishments: management of the establishment.

2-   Donations and alms shall be collected in closed boxes, which fulfill the following conditions :

a-   They shall bear the society's logo.

b-   To adhere to the specifications set up by the Department for the donations collection boxes.

c-   They shall be permanently placed at the mosques or in other places.

d-   The box shall have a serial number registered at the society.

e-   The person who collects donations for the society shall put an identification card in a clear place, bearing his photograph, his personal information and the society's logo.

f-   The places for the distribution of the boxes shall be known and registered by the society.

g-   The boxes allocated for the collection of Zakat shall be distinguished from boxes of alms and other donations.

h-   Collections of donations shall be made outside the mosque or at its external yard.

i-   The persons assigned to collect donations shall not raise their voices or insist on the donors and the members of the public, and the envelopes for collection of donations shall be placed beside the boxes.

j-   The boxes shall be opened by two persons at least, who shall count the money and record it in approved registers, before depositing the amounts in the society's account in the bank, provided the terms and conditions set up by the Department shall be adhered to.

k-

Donations collection procedures through
Banking transfers

Excerpts of the NGO Laws of the United Arab Emirates

Article (28):

Charitable societies may collect donations and alms from donors through banking transfers either in a continuous or non continuous manner.

The society shall submit a statement showing the amounts which were collected as required by the Department.

Donations collection procedures through Parties and charitable campaigns

Article (29):
The charitable societies shall adhere to the following conditions upon collection of cash and in kind donations through performance of parties and charitable campaigns and activities:

1-   To obtain permission from the Department, which determines the nature of the activity, its place and time.

2-   The nature of the activity shall take one of the following forms:
    a-   The charitable market.
    b-   The charitable campaign.
    c-   The charitable exhibition.
    d-   The religious presentation or lecture.

3-   The permission application shall state the names of the persons responsible for the management of the event and to receive the amounts collected from the donations of the public.

4- The society shall submit at the end of the campaign a statement showing the amounts, which were collected, if the Department requests so.

5- The same terms and conditions stipulated by article 27 of these rules shall be applied if donations are collected by boxes.

6-

Donations collection procedures through advertisements

Article (30):

The charitable society may collect donations through advertisements in the various advertisement media, provided that the advertisement shall not include any abuse to any certain party, or any violations to any of the applicable systems in this field.

Collection of donations through sponsorship

Article (31):

1- The charitable societies may collect donations through marketing of their events through the practice of sponsorship, provided they adhere to the following conditions:

a- The sponsoring company shall be licensed and registered by the concerned authorities

b- The objectives of the sponsorship shall be in agreement with the objectives of the society, which are stated in its articles of association

c- The sponsorship shall not contradict the principles of Islamic Sharia, the public morals, and the regulations applied in the State.

d- The society shall submit a statement at the end of the campaign showing the amounts which were collected, as required by the Department.

e- To submit a statement showing the method of spending these amounts.

2- If the sponsor is a company or an organization existing outside the State, which has no licensed branch inside the State, the society shall submit an application to the Department in order to obtain its prior approval.

Article (32):
The charitable society shall give priority to financing charitable activities inside the State, unless these amounts are the proceeds of a campaign or a donation dedicated for charitable purposes outside the State.

Article (33):
1-   The charitable societies shall spend their money for the achievement of their objectives. Their articles of association shows the methods of disposal of their money, and for management and keeping of them. The society shall adhere to the provisions included in these rules with respect to collection and spending of these amounts.

2-   The society shall undertake in determining its administrative expenses not to exceed the amount, which covers the minimum limit of these expenses, and such expenses shall not exceed 10% of the society's financial resources.

Article (34):
No other party apart from the charitable society may collect donations through sponsorship, unless they obtain a prior written approval from the Department, provided that they fulfill the following conditions:

1-   That party shall be a government department or an official establishment or a company licensed to work in the Emirate as per the law, and it may be an international organization, in which the State is a member.

2-   The organizing party shall submit an application to the Department including comprehensive information about the purpose of the collection of donations, the nature of the event or activity and how is it performed, the time and place of the event, and the other statements and conditions included in this article.

3-   The collection of donations shall be made through a charitable event or activity which does not contradict the provisions of Islamic Sharia, and shall not involve any Sharia violations, and shall not contradict the customs and traditions of the United Arab Emirates.

4-   The event shall be under the sponsorship of a charitable society licensed by the Department.

5-   A high ranking employee shall be assigned to be responsible for the supervision of collection of donations.

6-   To submit a final statement to the Department about the total collected donations, and the expenses incurred by the organizing committee as per official letters and reports.

7-   To adhere to any other conditions determined by the Department upon submitting the application. In case of violation of any conditions stipulated by this article, the establishment shall bear the consequences of legal accountability.

8-

Article (35):

No member of the board   of directors of the charitable societies or any of their employees shall be entitled to dispose of their funds, unless in the limit of achievement of their objectives as per the provisions of these rules, and the society's articles of association, in a manner, which does not contradict the society's internal regulations.

Article (36):
Those in charge of the affairs of any society may not issue a decision to dissolve it,   dispose of its movable or immovable properties, and its documents, unless by a resolution issued by the Department, or the concern authority, which shall determine the method of liquidation, and how to dispose of these properties and documents and the party to whom they shall belong.

Section two

Control of Religious and
Charitable Societies

Article (37):
The society shall provide the Department with any statement or information regarding its organizational affairs and its local or external activities, as requested, and this includes:

1-   The plans and annual work programs including its religious or charitable programs, and its annual budget.

2-   Its annual report including the final accounts, stating its financial resources, and methods of spending them.

3-   A statement of the names of persons whom the society intends to invite each year, to carry out its activities before one month at least from the date fixed for the performance of the activity. The statement shall include the subject of the activity, its date and a passport copy of the lecturer and his C.V, after obtaining the approval of the Department.

4-   Figures of the society's bank accounts with a letter authorizing the Department to inspect these accounts.

5-   The organizations which represent the society or cooperate with it outside the State.

6-   Events outside the State, which the society intends to perform.

7-   Regarding audio or reading or visual materials produced or distributed by the society, the society shall obtain permission from the Department to produce or print any of these materials before their production.

Article (38):
The Department shall follow up the financial procedures of the societies as follows:

1-   Verification of the sources of financing the societies, and that they are as per the provisions of the approved rules.

2-   Auditing the societies ' final accounts.

3-   Coordination with the banks to make sure of the financial resources of the societies, and the parties to whom these amounts were paid and to harmonize the same.

4-   To send delegates to the parties to whom the societies' funds are directed to verify that assistance has reached those parties or individuals, and that they are entitled and do not represent any violation to the provisions of charitable work.

If it is discovered for the Department that the financial performance of the society is weak, the Department may suggest systems, or rules or policies or financial procedures or technical programs to assist the society to manage it financial resources efficiently.

Article (39):
The Department shall carry out all the necessary procedures to ensure the efficiency of the administrative organization of the society, and the efficiency of its performance, and i

order to achieve that it may request the society to provide it with the necessary statements and information, and the Department shall verify the following in particular:

1- Names of employees, their personal and professional information, whether they work full time or part time or as volunteers.

2- The organizational structure, and the specializations and assignments of the administrative units.

3- Internal rules and instructions, and operational work guides.

4- The Department is entitled to address the general assembly or the parties responsible for appointment, suggesting changing the board of directors by another management, and to propose regulations, rules, organizational structures, guides and procedures, to upgrade the level of its management performance, upon the existence of practices conflicting with the applicable rules or regulations in the Emirate or the State.

Article (40):
The Department shall control the societies' activities by its administrative bodies, and may seek the assistance of any of the other concerned authorities in the Emirate, in performing its control duties as per the nature of the subject and its available capabilities.

Article (41):
If it is discovered to the Department that the society does not cooperate with it as per the articles stipulated by the rules, the Department shall be entitled to withdraw the license in coordination with the ministry or the concerned party. The Department shall be entitled also to refer those in charge of the society to the concerned departments, if it is discovered that they violated the objectives stipulated by the society's articles of association or the rules which regulate the work.

Section three
Violations and punishment

Article (42):
The society shall be considered as a violator if it commits any of the following actions:

1-   Violation of the provisions of laws, the rules regulating the activities of public benefit societies, and law # (12) for the year 2005 regarding the formation of Islamic Affairs & Chartable Activities Department, and the rules issued by it, or the violation of the society's articles of association.

2-   To commit any of the prohibited actions stipulated by these rules or any other resolutions issued by the Department.

Excerpts of the NGO Laws of the United Arab Emirates

3- Misuse of the society's funds or mismanagement of the same, thus squandering the available funds or misusing them, or creating indebtedness to the society.

4- Poor management performance of the societies, due to violation of internal rules or due to the bad selection of human resources necessary for the work

5- Concealment of any financial statements or information requested by the Department, or to tamper with the same or to present misleading information.

6- Proof of causing material or moral damage to any other party.

7- To carry out the work without renewing the license, unless this is due to reasons beyond the control of the society.

8- Violation of any of the provisions of these rules.

All these violations are only examples, and the Department shall prepare detailed rules including the violations and the resulting punishments.

Article (43):
The complaints against the society shall be filed to the Department from the following parties:

1- The concerned authority.

2- One of the employees or one of the members of the society's board of directors.

3- One member of the public.

4-   One employee of the Department.

These complaints shall be accompanied by evidence and the documents, which prove the case.

Article (44):
The Department shall do the following:

1-   To consider the complaint, and to carryout the necessary investigations, and to call the violator if it is an individual, or the representative of the society if necessary, or any other person or party whom the Department requires his presence.

2-   To decide the complaint and to forward the recommendation for the appropriate action, or to refer the violating person or party to the concerned authority.

Section four

Provisions for the formation of Foreign Communities Societies

Article (45):
The member of the society formed in the Emirate of Dubai by individuals representing one of the Islamic communities residing in the Emirate, shall fulfill the following conditions:

1-   He shall be conducting commercial or professional activities in the State.

2-   He shall have full legal civil capacity.

3-   His age shall not be less than twenty one years.

4-   He shall have good conduct, and shall not be convicted by an imprisonment sentence, unless he is pardoned and reinstated.

Article (46):
The founders shall meet as a constituent assembly to set up the society's articles of association, which shall include the following:

1-   Name and objectives of the society, and the community it represents.

2-   Names of the founding members, their surnames, age, nationality, occupation and place of residence.

3-   Membership conditions, its types, procedures for acceptance and cancellation of the same, and the rights and duties of members.

4-   Method of formation of the board of directors, its responsibilities, system of its sessions and its method of taking decisions.

5-   Rules for the organization of the meetings of the ordinary and extra -ordinary general assembly, its calling procedures, and conditions for its valid convening, and its responsibilities.

6-   Resources of the society and how to utilizes and dispose of them, and the method of controlling their spending, and the beginning and end of its fiscal year.

7- Conditions for the optional dissolution of the society, and rules for its liquidation.

Article (47):

The society shall keep at its head office the following records and documents:

1- The register of names of members and the subscriptions they pay.

2- Minutes of the board of directors, and its committees.

3- Revenues and expenses accounts supported by the documents.

All these records and documents shall bear the society's name.

Excerpts of the NGO Laws of the United Arab Emirates

Board of directors of communities societies,
and their general assembly

Article (48):
1-   The society formed by the communities shall have a
      board of directors whose members shall not be less than
      five persons to be selected by the general assembly for
      the period of three years, and any of its members may be
      re selected for similar periods.

2-   The society's articles of association shall determine the
      responsibilities of its board of directors, and the
      conditions which shall be available in its members,
      number of members, method of their selection and
      cancellation of their membership, procedures for calling
      the general assembly, and conditions for the validity of
      its meetings and resolutions.

Article (49):
1-   The society's general assembly shall consist of all its
      members as per its articles of association; the meeting of
      the general assembly shall be valid if more than half the
      members at least attend before the start of the meeting.

2-   If the required number is not available, the meeting shall
      be adjourned to the next day, and the meeting shall be
      valid in this case if a quarter of the members at least
      attend it.

3-   If the required member Is not available for this meeting
      in the next day, the chairman of the society's board of
      directors shall be entitled to request the Department to
      authorize the board of directors to exercise the powers of
      the general assembly for a period determined by the

authorization resolution, provided that the period shall not exceed six months.

Article (50):

The general assembly shall convene its ordinary meeting once a year within the three months following the end of fiscal year to discuss the following matters:

1- Approval of the minutes of the previous meeting.

2- Approval of the report of the board of directors about its work during the past year and of the society's programs and its action plan for the New Year.

3- Approval of the balance sheet for the past fiscal year and the budget project for the next fiscal year.

4- Selection of the new board of directors upon the end of the term of the previous board, or if there are vacant positions in the board.

5- Appointment of the accounts auditor.

6- Other matters included in the agenda.

The general assembly issues its resolutions by the majority of the votes of the attending members.

Article (51):

The general assembly may be called to convene extra ordinary meetings as per the request of the Department, which states the reasons for the call, or from the society's board of directors, or as per a request submitted by a quarter of the members entitled to attend the general assembly.

Excerpts of the NGO Laws of the United Arab Emirates

Article (52):
The extra ordinary general assembly shall discuss the following matters:

1- To decide the resignations submitted by all or part of the members of the board, or cancellation of their membership, and filling of the vacant positions.

2- Amendment of the society's articles of association.

3- Optional dissolution of the society.

4- Other important and urgent matters.
5-
The resolutions of the general assembly shall be passed in these cases by the majority of two thirds of the attending members.

Dissolution of community societies

Article (53):
1-   The Department shall dissolve the society formed by the communities in the following cases:

a- If its members are less than the limit stated in article (15) of these rules.

b- If it is found out that its works do not achieve its objectives, or if it becomes incapable of achieving these objectives.

c- If it disposes of its funds in purposes, contrary to those which are originally stipulated.

d- If it becomes unable to fulfill its financial obligations.

e- If it does not keep its records and documents according to article 47 of these rules, or if such records willfully contain incorrect statements.

f- If the society commits a serious violation of the provisions of these rules or of its articles of association.

This shall be without prejudice to referring the case to the concerned authority to take the legal procedures.

Nevertheless, the Department is entitled to call the extra ordinary meeting of the general assembly to elect a new board of directors. The Department is entitled to change the board of directors as it sees fit, through coordination with the general assembly or the official appointment departments or the ministry.

Article (54):
Adhering to the provisions of the previous article, the society may be optionally dissolved by a resolution of the extra ordinary general assembly, provided that the Department shall be notified about the place of the meeting before fifteen days at least from the date of the meeting.

Section five
General provisions

Article (55):
The society which is existing at the time of applying this rules shall amend its articles of association according to the provisions of these rules within six months from the date of their application, otherwise the society shall be considered as illegal, and the Department may address the concerned authority to take the necessary action against it.

Excerpts of the NGO Laws of the United Arab Emirates

Article (56):
The society shall issue internal rules to regulate its work and to form any committees belonging to it, provided that this does not contradict the laws of the state or the provisions of these rules or the society's articles of association.

Article (57):
The Department shall be entitled to attend the meetings of the general assembly and to review the minutes of the sessions of the board of directors, and its ordinary and extra ordinary general assembly.

Article (58):
These rules shall be effective from their issue date, and shall be circulated to the concerned parties.

The general manager

These rules are issued in Dubai.
Date 23/11/1426 H
Corresponding to: 23/1/2006

REFERENCES

Acts of 1966, State Library of Massachusetts, November 16, 2008, available at http://archives.lib.state.ma.us/actsResolves/1966/1966acts042 1.pdf.

Annan, Kofi. April 12, 2000. "Secretary-General, in Havana on Eve of First 'Group of 77' Summit Meeting, Evokes Promises and Pitfalls of Globalization" in *UN Press Release*. SG/SM/7357.

Barros, John. 2001. "Youth Leadership Development: A Space, a Voice and Some Power." The Nonprofit Quarterly, Vol. 8, Issue 4.

Cernea, M. M. 1984. *Putting People First*. Oxford Reprint Paperback.

Chenery, H. B. 1961. Comparative Advantage and Economic Policy.

Community Land Trust Model. Institute for Community Economics, November 16, 1008, available at http://www.iceclt.org/clt/cltmodel.html.

Copestake, James. "Theories of Economic Development 1999." *UNESCO Encyclopedia of Life Sciences* (draft artcle), available at http://staff.bath.ac.uk/hssjgc/unesco.html#Sec2

Danson, Michael and Geoff Whittam. 1999. *Regional Governance, Institutions and Development*. Regional Research Institute, West Virginia Univeristy.

Dervis, Kemal et. al. *Yemen - Toward a Water Strategy: An Agenda for Action* (World Bank, Aug. 1997).

"Development Cooperation." Embassy of the Kingdom of the Netherlands in Sana'a, Republic of Yemen, November 16, 2008, available at http://yemen.nlembassy.org/development.

Dorn, James A. 1998. *The Revolution in Development Economics*. Washington Cato Institute Press.

Dudley Street Neighborhood Initiative, November 16, 2008, available at http://www.dsni.org.

Dulles, Allen (1994) *The Marshall Plan*. Berg Publishers.

Easterly, W. "Does Foreign Aid Really Add Up." *Journal of Economic Growth, December 2000.*

Easterly, W. 1997. The Ghost of Financing Gap: How the Harrod Domar Growth Model Still Haunts Development Economic.

Fitch, Rober. "The cooperative economics of Italy's Emilia-Romagna holds a lesson for the U.S. In Bologna, Small is Beautiful." *The Nation*. May 13, 1996.

Frankel, S. Herert. 1952. United Nations Primer on Development.

Freedom in the World. Freedom House, Nov. 1, 2008, available at http://www.freedomhouse.org/.

Gerrard, Michael B. "Public-Private Partnerships." *Finance and Development: A Quarterly Magazine of the IMF* (International Monetary Fund, Sept. 2001).

Guislain, Pierre. The Privatization Challenge: A Strategic, Legal, and Institutional Analysis of International Experience (World Bank, 1997).

References

Harris, Seymour Edwin. 1972. Economic Problems of Latin America.

Hull, Cordell (1948). *The Memoirs of Cordell Hull*. New York: Macmillan.

The Human Development Concept. United Nations Development Programme, Nov. 1, 2008, available at http://hdr.undp.org/en/humandev/.

Johnson, D. G. 1997. "Agriculture and the Wealth of Nations." *The American Economic Review*, Vol. 87, No. 2, May 1997, pages 1-12.

Keynes, John Maynard. 1940. *How to Pay for the War*. London.

Keys to Successful Public-Private Partnerships. The National Council for Public-Private Partnerships, 30 Oct. 2007, available at http://www.ncppp.org/howpart/index.shtml#keys.

Leaf. M. 2004. "The Green Revolution." *The Encyclopedia of Environmental History*. Shepard Krech III, J. R. McNeill and Carolyn Merchant, eds. New York and London: Routlege. Vol 2:615-619.

Leaf, M. J. 1981. "The Green Revolution in a Punjab Village: 1964-1978." *Economic Development and Cultural Change*.

Logue, John. 2006 *Economics and Cooperation: The Emilia Romagna Model*. OurBiz International. December 10, 2006.

Mabel Louise Riley Foundation, November 16, 2008, available at http://www.rileyfoundation.com.

Marshall, George. 1947. *Speech Delivered by General George Marshall at Harvard University on June 5, 1947*. Modern History Sourcebook, Nov. 09, 2008, available at

http://www.fordham.edu/halsall/mod/1947marshallplan1.ht
ml.

McKinzie, Richard D. 1974. "Oral History Interview with John
Wesley Jones". Harry S. Truman Library & Museum, Nov. 9,
2008, available at
http://www.trumanlibrary.org/oralhist/jonesjw.htm.

Medoff, Peter, and Holly Sklar. *Streets of Hope: The Fall and Rise of an
Urban Neighborhood.* Published by Peter Medoff and Holly Sklar,
1994.

Milich, Lenard and Mohammed Al-Sabbry. *The "Rational Peasant"
vs Sustainable Livelihoods: The Case of Qat in Yemen.* The
University of Arizona, 1995.

Mises, Ludwig von. 1934. *Theory of Money and Credit.* London.

The Money Lenders. The World Bank & International Monetary
Fund: A Global Report. (film)

Neal, W.C. 1990. "Absolute Cultural Relativism: Firm Foundation
for Valuing and Policy." *Journal of Economic Issues*, 0021-3624,
June 1, 1990, Vol. 24, Issue 2.

*A Partnership Approach to Sustainable Groundwater Management in
Yemen.* Ministry of Water and Environment, Yemen. Fourth
World Water Forum, Mexico, March, 2006.

Participation and Civic Engagement. The World Bank, November 12,
2008, available at http://www.worldbank.org/participation.

Project Performance Assessment Report: Yemen. World Bank, Feb.
2006, Report No. 35004.

References

Ranis, Gustav. 2004. Arthur Lewis' Contribution to Development Thinking and Policy. Yale University, available at http://www.rh.edu/~stodder/BE/Lewis_byRanis.htm.

Rome Declaration on World Food Security.

Rostow, W. W. 1956. The Take-Off to Self-Sustained Growth.

Sahooly, Anwer. "Public-Private Partnership in the Water Supply and Sanitation Sector: The Experience of the Republic of Yemen." *International Journal of Water Resources Development* (Routledge, June 2003).

Sicherman, Harvey. 1998. "America and the West: Lessons from the Marshall Plan". Watch on the West: A Newsletter of FPRI's Center for the Study of America and the West, January 1998, Vol. 1, No. 3.

Special Unit for South-South Cooperation. United Nations Development Programme, 30 Oct. 2007, available at http://www.ncppp.org/undp/index.html.

Stiglitz, Joseph E. 2003. *Globalization and Its Discontents.* W. W. Norton & Company.

Stiglitz, Joseph E. 2006. *Making Globalization Work.* W. W. Norton & Company.

Thompson, David J. 2003. Italy's *Emilia Romagna: Clustering Co-op Development.* Cooperative Grocer: For Retailers and Cooperators. No. 109.

Universal Declaration of Human Rights. United Nations, Nov. 1, 2008, available at http://www.un.org/Overview/rights.html.

Urban Revitalization Corporations, Chapter 121A, General Law of Massachusetts. November 16, 2008, available at http://www.mass.gov/legis/laws/mgl/gl-121a-toc.htm.

USAID: About USAID. U.S. Agency for International Development, Nov. 1, 2008, available at http://www.usaid.gov/about_usaid/.

Van Ginneken, Meike. *Improving Performance through Bilateral Utility Partnerships*. World Bank Water Operators Partnership Workshop, Johannesburg, April 2007.

Vanhanen, Tatu. 2000. *Polyarchy Dataset Manuscript*. International Peace Research Institute, Oslo. Available at http://www.prio.no/CSCW/Datasets/Governance/Vanhanens-index-of-democracy/Polyarchy-Dataset-Manuscript/.

Vogler, Justin. "Democratising globalisation: Joseph Stiglitz interviewed". *Open Democracy: Free Thinking for the World* (September 2006). Available at http://www.opendemocracy.net/globalization-vision_reflections/stiglitz_3931.jsp.

Williamson, Jeffrey G. 1985. The Historical Content of the Classical Labor Surplus Model.

Yemen. World Bank, November 14, 2008, available at http://web.worldbank.org/WBSITE/EXTERNAL/COUNTRIES/MENAEXT/YEMENEXTN/0,,menuPK:310170~pagePK:141159~piPK:141110~theSitePK:310165,00.html.

Yemen Country Profile: Natural Resources. United Nations Development Programme, Yemen, 30 Oct. 2007, available at http://www.undp.org.ye/resources.php.

References

Yemen - Project Appraisal Document for the First Phase of the Urban Water Supply & Sanitation Program. World Bank, July, 2002, Report No. 24478-YEM.

Yemen: World Bank to Upgrade Water Supply, Sanitation Services. World Bank, August 1, 2002, Press Release No. 2002/040/MENA.

BIOGRAPHICAL INFORMATION

Alexandra De Vito graduated *cum laude* from the College of Architecture and Planning, Ball State University Honors College, prior to beginning her Masters of City and Regional Planning at the School of Urban and Public Affairs of the University of Texas at Arlington. As a Project Architect licensed in the State of Texas, she has seven years of experience with the firm Corgan Associates, Inc. Her particular interest in city planning as it relates to development has taken her to renovation and outreach projects in nations as diverse as Belize, Egypt, Kenya, Mexico, and most recently, the United Arab Emirates. She has been named Research Fellow of the American Institute for Yemeni Studies to undertake research on public private partnerships in Yemen.

John Balouziyeh is a dual common law / civil law-qualified attorney, having completed his legal studies at Universidad Abat Oliba in Barcelona and Regent University School of Law in Virginia. While he was a graduate student at L'Institut d'Études Politiques de Paris (Sciences Po) and a Fulbright Fellow in Turkey, his studies focused on the role that civil society, institution building and legal reform play in international development. As an attorney at the US Department of State, he rotated through the Abu Dhabi office of the U.S.-Middle East Partnership Initiative (MEPI), which supports public-private partnerships with civil society organizations throughout the Middle East and North Africa to promote political, economic and social reform.